OPENING *to* GOD

Childlike Prayers for Adults

Marilyn McCord Adams

Westminster John Knox Press
LOUISVILLE • LONDON

Book design by Drew Stevens
Cover design by Pam Poll Graphic Design

First edition
Published by Westminster John Knox Press
Louisville, Kentucky

This book is printed on acid-free paper that meets the American National Standards Institute Z39.48 standard. ♾

PRINTED IN THE UNITED STATES OF AMERICA

08 09 10 11 12 13 14 15 16 17 — 10 9 8 7 6 5 4 3 2 1

Library of Congress Cataloging-in-Publication Data

Adams, Marilyn McCord.
    Opening to God : childlike prayers for adults / Marilyn McCord Adams. — 1st ed,
      p. cm.
    Includes index.
    ISBN 978-0-664-23305-1 (alk. paper)
    1. Prayers. I. Title.

BV245.A36 2008
242'.8—dc22

                                                                2007050511

CONTENTS

INTRODUCTION

IDENTIFYING THE GENRE

When I speak of prayer in this book, I use the word broadly for *personal sharing between human beings and God*. Personal communication comes in many forms. The most profound is (more or less) *undefended personal presence*. This is found with infants who have no defenses and with children who are just learning how to build them. It is found with friends who deliberately lower their defenses to share themselves more deeply. It is found with lovers who are swept off their feet and stare into one another's eyes for hours without saying anything. It is found with life partners and companions who are habitually so available to each other, who know each other so well, that they can communicate without saying anything. Person-to-person presence enables infants and children to become themselves and adults to get to know not only the other but also themselves. Becoming and knowing oneself and getting to know the other are deeply intertwined.

Normally, personal presence is not the only mode of communication among human beings. Because we are *rational* animals, we are language users. Birds may sing and donkeys bray, but our human calling is to express our experience of the world in articulate speech. Moreover, because we are *personal* animals, we are meaning makers. God honors this when (Gen. 2:18–24) God invites Adam to name the animals, to share with God the work of conferring significance, of helping to define what things mean. The story also shows this happening between human persons. For human beings, it is not enough simply to *be* together. We want to *declare* who we are and what we mean to each other. Jesus models our need for this: "Who do they . . . who do you say that I am?" (Matt. 16:13–23//Mark 8:27–33//Luke 9:18–22). Instinctively, we respond to one another with the daily questions "Who do you say that we are? What do we mean to you? What do you think we mean?"

For most of us, language is learned before it is invented. We are born with a growing capacity for speech. We learn to talk in stages, copycatting the speakers around us as best we can. In the beginning, adults babble at babies, who eventually learn to imitate the monosyllables and "goo" and "gah" back. Crawlers and toddlers learn names and progress to one-word assertions, reactions, and demands: "Truck!" (for "There goes a truck!" and/or "I want to ride in the truck"); "No!"; "More!" ("Please give me some more!"); "Up!" ("Please pick me up!"); and so forth. Next come simple sentences followed by more complex ones. School-age children move from narratives that tell "one damn thing after the other" to stories with dramatic structure, plot tension, and resolution. Overall, linguistic development runs alongside and expands with cognitive and emotional development until the individual reaches adult-level skills.

Because human personality is highly vulnerable, we normally reach adulthood armed with a variety of psychospiritual defenses that are consciously and unconsciously triggered to allow us to be more or less personally present as the situation requires. Words become all the more important because of their flexibility. Words allow us to communicate with one another efficiently enough to "get the job done" despite high levels of personal reserve. Language itself signals levels of formality and familiarity and thus serves to set the tone. Most interactions involve a mixture of personal presence and verbal communication. Back and forth, the one can give way to the other, or can interpret, reinforce, or belie the other.

Personal communication with God is in many ways analogous. There is *wordless presence*. God is omnipresent by nature. But our wordless presence to God, our special openness to God that makes us able to discern the divine presence that always surrounds us, is more occasional. Just as a mother's presence to an infant affects the child's psyche before the child has any conscious capacities, drawing the child into the self-consciousness that enables it to be a person, divine omnipresence affects us psycho-spiritually, drawing us into focus as spiritual persons capable of reaching out to others, able to make contact even with God. Just as adult openness to others is partly voluntary and partly involuntary, so is our openness to divine presence. Just as we can learn ways deliberately to open ourselves to or put up defenses against other persons, so we can develop ways to wall God out, to keep God at arm's length, or to unlock our heart's doors. Many valuable books on wordless prayer take their cues from great contemplative or mystical writers.

By contrast, this book focuses on prayer as it involves *verbal* communication. It is a collection of prayers that model verbal communication of a certain style and from a certain posture: that of adults responding to Jesus' invitation to enter the kingdom of heaven like children (Matt. 18:3//Mark 10:15//Luke 18:17). I envision children between seven and ten years old, who have a good command of language and a basic orientation to the world around them, but who are not yet civilized into adult inhibitions. I have in mind children who are curious and teachable, who are beginning to learn enough to have a sense of what they do not already know, but who are not yet jaded and still want to discover more. I think of children who feel no need to pretend to know more than they do or to be more competent than they are, children who feel no pressure to pose as paragons who need no improvement. I imagine children who are alert to incongruities, who are sensitive to misfits, who notice when things don't add up. I picture children who experience no need to hide even if they have to some extent learned to control their emotions: children who feel safe enough to display their wounds, to expose their weakness and fear, to express their anger, and to admit their mistakes.

Equally important, I envision children who trust adults enough to challenge and question and who do so expecting adults to be able to help. Children eventually learn to be cagey because adults are insecure. Because the children depend on the adults' goodwill, children have to stay in their good graces by keeping them calm and comfortable, by helping them to save face. Much etiquette is designed for just this purpose. Once young people have learned that it is not safe to be candid, they have begun to leave childhood behind.

My hypothesis (based on personal and pastoral experience) is that people tend to project such etiquette onto the heavens. Implicitly, God becomes for us an insecure authority figure whose face we have to save by restricting ourselves to nonthreatening, euphemistic, polite conversation. Service books such as the *Book of Common Prayer* get treated as the Emily Post or Miss Manners of prayer practice, authoritative manuals instructing us in the approved terms of flattery and self-deprecation and furnishing models of how to frame unpleasant subjects and manage conflicts. It is the theology voiced by Job's friends: we had better not "sin with the lips" if we know what's good for us!

The trouble is, this theological picture is false. God *is* supremely authoritative. But for that very reason, God is too big to be shrunk down to a "Jack and the Bean Stalk," giant-sized version of our merely human authority figures. Unconsciously imagining God this way is the real insult because it paints God much too small! Nor is this really the doctrine promulgated by official denominational worship books. The familiar and beloved *Book of Common Prayer* and its analogues contain services of *public* worship. Their "one-size-fits-all" language is suited to *formal* occasions, the better to accomodate and accompany many types of people through the chances and changes of this present life. In our society, formal ceremonies and official occasions still claim an important place. For this purpose, such worship books furnish apt script and choreography.

My point is that if this is the *only* way we relate to God, the only tone of voice or style of communication we use, our relationship with God will be impoverished. We would be like royal children who never interacted with their parents except in official court ceremonies! God would be to us an aloof stranger or touchy authority figure with whom we have to be careful. But what we want and need is a God who also relates to us as father or mother or friend or personal trainer, someone who demands a lot of us but also someone in whom it is safe to confide. We need a God with whom we can be candid about our weaknesses and limitations as well as our hopes and dreams, a God whom we can trust to stick with us and help us to grow.

Put otherwise, relating to God only formally and officially trains us to approach God with our psychospiritual defenses up, which cuts us off from *experiencing* the omnipresent love that surrounds us. Yet, the felt touch of that love is just what we need to gain confidence that God is *for* us, to become convinced that boundless goodness utterly outclasses all created goods and ills, to stir the heart's expectation that—come hell or high water—

God will make everything all right! By contrast, greeting God through the unrent veil of our defenses confirms our sense that as adults we are on our own in what may be euphemistically described as a challenging environment, that we must pull ourselves together, make the best of it, and hope that God (like the commander in chief) will recognize a job well done. Whatever our head continues to believe, whatever liturgical formulas we may repeat, turning God into the ultimate line manager, who keeps books on our outputs, dims our hopes into stoic resolve.

Jesus recommends the antidote: undo these habits of reserve by becoming as a little child. Of course, adults are not children. Adults are in many ways more sensitive and sophisticated. Adult experience of the world is wider, richer, and more complex. Jesus is not saying that a good relationship with God requires adults to regress and become naive and simplistic. Rather the recommended spiritual exercise involves a "developmental double take." Prayer is personal sharing with God. The content to be shared is our adult experience of life in this world, but we are to share it with God the way a child would: with candor and vulnerability, with emotional immediacy, with curiosity and teachability, and with a knife-edge balance between demand and expectation of tender loving care, constructive criticism, and friendly help.

What keeps developmental double take from constituting conduct unbecoming to adults is the "size gap" between God and creatures. God is very, very big, and we are very, very small. Julian of Norwich explains that God's personal capacities so outclass humans' that even the most mature human beings are like infants or toddlers in comparison. In this world, even highly competent adults cannot manage sometimes. Human affairs can get radically out of hand. We and those we love can take big hits.

Events can leave us stunned, not knowing what to make of them or how to recover. Childlike prayer is a way of sharing the ups and downs, the disappointments and delights, the disastrous failures and wrenching losses, the satisfactions and sweet successes, all the twists and turns of our lives with God, the boundless love who creates us, who has given us a difficult assignment by making us in this world, but who wants to help us, and, above all, to collaborate with us on a common task.

For a biblical example of an adult who practices childlike prayer, we need look no further than Job. When Job loses wealth, health, and offspring, his first response is pious: "The Lord gives, the Lord takes away. Blessed be the name of the Lord!" As his suffering deepens, Job protests that he has done nothing to deserve it and charges God with wrong: either divine wisdom and cosmos-organizing powers are lacking, or God is unfair. God is more like a chaos monster than a creator. God slays the innocent with the guilty. Job's appalled "friends" are afraid of being counted guilty by association with such blasphemy. They draw on every conventional theological theme they can think of to defend God by blaming the victim. Failing to win a sympathetic hearing from his friends, Job concludes that God is more trustworthy than they are. For chapters, Job pours out his suffering, telling God in no uncertain terms just how bad things look and feel to him. For chapters, God holds back, veiling divine presence so that Job won't be too intimidated to speak his mind. Then, when Job has fully vented his indignation and misery, God addresses him out of the whirlwind and shares God's contrasting point of view. God vindicates Job for telling more truth than his friends did. Job has to admit, he was wrong to accuse God of incompetence. And, because Job's rant against God was uninhibited, his defenses are all the way down, and he sees God face to face.

THIS BOOK AND ITS USES

The prayers in this book are grouped under three headings. Part 1, "Opening the Self to God," begins with prayers that express our difficulties in knowing how to pray and ask for God's help and patience. It moves on to prayers that spill out our personal worries and obsessions, our struggles with suffering, our pain and fear and bewilderment in journeying towards death. Next come prayers that talk about our relationships with friends and enemies and members of our households. Prayers that confess our failures are followed by expressions of appreciation for the good things of life. Part 1 closes with prayers that expose both the astonishment and the stress that go with collaborating with God.

Part 2, "Faith Seeking Understanding," gathers prayers that "come out of the closet" to God with our questions. Received pictures of God don't fit with our experience of ourselves and the world. Proposed explanations don't make sense. Standard theological arguments leave gaping holes. These prayers follow Job's example in taking our observations and complaints, our frustration, confusion, and possible insights "straight to the top" by laying them out before God.

Christian faith speaks of the Bible as God's word: the written text of the Bible is a medium of God's message, which the Holy Spirit in our hearts enables us to understand. If so, we can think of Bible reading as starting a conversation with God. The Bible stories and teachings convey a message about who God is, how God acts, and what God wants or expects of us. Our prayer continues the conversation by responding to what we heard in what was said. Just as it is natural to ask human friends or teachers for clarification or explanation, to inquire how what they just said fits with their remarks on other occasions, to raise apparent counterexamples, and to probe for how their claims might apply to particular situations in life, so it is with God. God is our Teacher and is sure to understand our predicament. After all, the Bible is a library of books that reflect human cultures very different from our own, stretching across seventeen hundred years. Even to a believer who has read it repeatedly, who has pored over many and various commentaries, the Bible is not easy to understand. Winning through to its meaning and relevance for us is a spiritual exercise that lasts a lifetime. Praying the Bible instead of pretending we have no problems with it is a way to seek help from the best informed source and thus open ourselves to understand better what God has in mind.

Part 3, "Caring for God's World," moves beyond individual concerns to the wider world, to events and problems that we read about in the newspaper and perhaps encounter in our working lives. At least since 9/11, terrorist attacks have been on the increase. Part 3 begins with prayers that share our terror with God. A few of these mention particular incidents (the 9/11 attacks in the United States and the 7/7 London bombings), but are easily adaptable to other events. Because current terrorism exploits ethnic and religious divisions, prayers about terrorism are followed with those that acknowledge our racism and prejudice. Our experience of violence also prompts prayers for peace and good governments. Next come prayers about social injustice and the condition of prisoners. Churches are also institutions with important social functions as well as crises and problems that cry out for prayers. Finally, there are prayers about our concern for the environment and our stewardship of planet earth.

This collection of prayers can be used privately as a kind of spiritual exercise book that helps to shift its user into the practice of childlike prayer. For this purpose, it is best to try one or a few prayers on topics that seem apt at the time. Because personal communication moves back and forth between verbal communication and wordless presence, it works well to adopt a meditative pace. After all, the prayers open by sharing our perspective with God. Courtesy requires a pause that waits to receive what God might be sharing in return. Sometimes there is a figure/ground shift in our perspective that will provoke new questions and observations. The prayers in this collection are offered as models. The point is not to stick with the samples but to "get the hang of it" and launch out on one's own.

In fact, most of these prayers were written for and used in public worship at Christ Church, Oxford. Our cathedral gets many tourists for choral evensong. Some are observant Christians, but many are not. While music transcends barriers of language and culture, there is a real question as to how well the spoken part of our service communicates with those who attend. We use the 1662 *Book of Common Prayer* service with its old-fashioned English. Our lectionary divides the text in strange ways and serves up Bible stories for which hearers have little or no context. On weekdays, time constraints rule out a homily. But there is room after the anthem for three collects chosen by the canon in residence. I came to see these as an opportunity to speak in another voice and to try to convey the relevance of what we had just done in another way. Doubtless the prayers I composed would work even better in public services that use contemporary language throughout.

To make it easier to use the prayers, biblical references are attached at the end of each one. In the section "Praying the Bible," the reference is to a passage directly engaged by the prayer. Prayers in the other sections also contain biblical allusions that are more thematic. To help correlate prayers with readings used in public worship, sample passages are given following the prayer. The prayers are numbered and indexed by that number in the topical index and in the index of biblical passages.

Over time, I got more comments on these prayers than I did on any of my sermons. People reported themselves moved, surprised, provoked, or startled. It seemed that the prayers had touched something. My guess is that it touched their own desire to be childlike with God.

Marilyn McCord Adams
Christ Church, Oxford

PART ONE
OPENING THE SELF TO GOD

Trying to Pray

1 O God, you know everything. Reading minds and hearts is easy for you. What's hard for us is to know how to share ourselves willingly. Like infants in mothers' arms, we need you to teach us. Give us the language. Stir up the trust. Kindle the desire to know even as we are known. Through Jesus Christ. Amen.

Luke 11:1–13; 18:1

2 O God, we think we want to keep your company. But we're so different, your ways so much higher than our ways, that it's hard to know how to take a step in your direction. We put our bodies in the pew, shape our mouths around the words, stand and bow and kneel the way the book tells us. But often you seem so strange to us that we leave bewildered, not knowing whether we've pleased you or not. O God, we're so different, your ways so much higher than our ways, that we'll never get together unless you're tolerant. Help us to trust you enough to experiment. Overcome our fears with desire. Through Jesus Christ. Amen.

Isa. 55:6–9; Luke 11:1–13

3 O God, you are everywhere and always. You made us with hearts of flesh to feel, with spirits sensitive to perceive your love and power. But we learned long ago that we can't afford to pay attention to everything. Too many facts confuse us. Especially other people's needs and desires complicate our picture and make it too difficult to get everything under control. Consciously and unconsciously, we have spent our lives building defenses, setting up filters to limit what we have to acknowledge. So here we are, self-made people leading twisted lives in half-baked worlds. O God, sneak through the walls that divide us. Make your touch unmistakable. Restore our sense of what is really real. Through Jesus Christ. Amen.

Isa. 7:10–16; Ezek. 36:26; Mark 8:14–26

4 O God, sometimes you crash through our everyday way of living in the world with a presence so impressive that we can't deny your really, really Realness, so bright that we can simply *see* how radically you outclass everything else. But precisely because you do, we don't know how to fit you into our everyday picture. You explode any roles we try to assign you. You are too different from everything else. So we set you and our experiences of you to one side, because if we took who you are into account, you might turn our worlds inside out, upside down, and backwards. O God, you know how much stability we need. You know how little uncertainty we can tolerate. Teach us how to live in *your* world. Help us to feel safe because you are in charge. Through Jesus Christ. Amen.

Exod. 14:19; 34:27–35; Job 38–42; Isa. 6:1–8; 7:10–16; Luke 5:1–11; 24; John 20–21; Matt. 17:1–8//Mark 9:2–8//Luke 9:28–36

5 O God, the magi in the story looked for the newborn king in a palace, and we seek you out by coming to church. At least from time to time, we expect to find you in

the midst of music, to greet your real presence at Holy Communion, to hear your Word to us in a sermon. O God, open us up to notice you in street people selling magazines, in citizens caught in cross fires of war and ethnic conflicts, in children hungering for education or just safe shelter and regular food. Help us to recognize your voice in our critics, to be startled into learning from those most different from us. O God, heal our blindness and deafness until we perceive your dazzle—holiness all around! Through Jesus Christ. Amen.

Matt. 2:1–12; 15:21–28; 25:31–46; Luke 10:25–37; Matt. 11:7–15// Luke 7:24–30

6 O God, that injunction to love you with all of our heart, soul, strength, and mind can seem pretty demanding. But to tell the truth, there is so much to you and so little to us that it takes all of our powers brought into sharp focus to pay attention to you. On our own, we can't seem to manage it for more than a minute. Even when we do get a glimpse, we can't steady our gaze. We feel overloaded and have to turn away. O God, we need your Holy Spirit to come and help us if we are ever going to see you face to face. Through Jesus Christ. Amen.

Deut. 6:4–5; Ps. 8; Matt. 22:37//Mark 12:29–30//Luke 10:27; Rom. 8:26–27

7 O God, we were taught from earliest childhood how we ought to respect our elders. Even now, think of the elaborate etiquette that has to be observed whenever someone meets foreign dignitaries or high government officials! Much as we love them, official service books easily give the impression that we should mind our manners and be especially selective about what we say to you. O God, thank you for examples like Job who show us how to blurt out what we really think and feel. Thank you for showing us how candor can be the first risk of trust, the first step towards love. Through Jesus Christ. Amen.

Exod. 20:12; Deut. 5:16; 27:16; Job 3; 7; 19

Sharing Our Worries, "Outing" Our Demons

8   O God, strengthen us in times of anxiety with serenity; in times of hardship, with courage; in times of perplexity, with wisdom; in times of frustration, with patience; and at all times, with confidence in your resourcefulness and love. Amen.

Matt. 6:25–34//Luke 12:22–34; Phil. 4:4–7; Jas. 1:2–12

9   O God, we go on trips for good reasons: to get away from it all, to escape the entanglements of daily life that get us down, to let our executive selves idle, and to open ourselves to fresh surprises. But when we actually get on the road, the journey has the vices of its virtues. Everything is unfamiliar. We easily panic because we don't at first recognize the things that will meet our needs. O God, stir up our memories of why we left home in the first place. Convince us that it is safe to follow where you lead us, for we are always traveling with you. Through Jesus Christ. Amen.

Num. 11:4–6; 14:1–3; 20:2–5

10 O God, you know how all of us want to find satisfying lives, ways of living and relating that engage our gifts, stretch us towards achievements, warm us with companionship, and reach out to include those who have been left out. But we don't know how to get our lives in balance. We work too hard and then fritter away time. We don't take lunch breaks and get fat on junk food. We withdraw from bad company, only to become desperate and embrace worse. Cut through our confusion to convince us of how much you've always loved us. Shape our approach to life, to ourselves and others, with the confidence that we are all loved very much by you. Through Jesus Christ. Amen.

Gal. 5:1, 13–25; Phil. 4:4–7; Col. 3:1–17; 1 Tim. 6:6–19

11 O God, sometimes we are so tired from overwork and stress and lack of sleep that it hurts physically. Perspective vanishes. Patience is exhausted. Flexibility is a thing of the past. One more obstacle is enough to make our task seem impossible and our way of life intolerable. O God, guide us through the maze of our busy-ness to your stillness at the center. Water us daily from the well of your calm. Through Jesus Christ. Amen.

Num. 11:10–30; Mark 6:30–46; Phil. 4:4–7

12 O God, when we were children, sleep seemed like a waste of time. Life was so full of interest and discovery that we couldn't see the point of going to bed. We didn't understand then that our bodies needed a break to gather energy to grow us up into bigger and more capable versions of ourselves. But now that we're adults, it's all reversed. We *feel* exhausted. We know our staying power isn't what it used to be. But work and worry produce insomnia that robs us of the rest we need. O God, pills and

sheep counting are not the answer. You sent dreams to the patriarchs. Come lullaby us into a good night's sleep. Through Jesus Christ. Amen.

Ps. 131

13 O God, you are with us through life and death. Make your presence known to all those caught up in the dangers and turmoil of war: soldiers who witness buddies blown to pieces and wonder whether their turn is next; men, women, and children huddling in their houses, afraid to go out for bread and olives, unable to sleep for the sound of exploding bombs and cars. O God, help them not to panic. Reassure them that violence cannot separate them from their life with you. Through Jesus Christ. Amen.

Ps. 46; 90; 121; 139; 2 Cor. 1:3–7

14 O God, normally, we're responsible people. We know how to pull ourselves together, shift into the achievement mode, and get things done. Normally, we have our wits about us. Normally, we are able to bring the full force of our insight to bear on problems and tasks that really matter. But sometimes we're seized with anxiety. We feel as if we're coming apart, as if our executive core has evaporated, as if all of our energy and skill are being sucked into a black hole. We panic with the fleeting recognition that we have no power in ourselves to help ourselves. O God, pull us out of the pit. Enable us to function, but convince us that our integrity depends on you. Through Jesus Christ. Amen.

Matt. 6:25–34//Luke 12:22–34; Phil. 4:4–7

15 O God, in many and various ways, human societies send the message that if you can't be useful to the

community, you really shouldn't use up resources or take up space. Sometimes, ancient societies literally abandoned the old or maimed or differently abled. Nowadays, we just cut pensions and social services to make sure they get the message of how they are so unwanted that they might as well die. O God, forgive us for degrading your image in others. Forgive us also for making you in our image, for fearing that you are out to degrade us as well. Through Jesus Christ. Amen.

Ps. 71:9; Luke 14:12–14

16 O God, we really want to belong to you, to be sheep of your flock and lambs of your redeeming. But sometimes we're afraid that you will leave us out in the cold. When we strain to listen but don't hear your voice, we worry that maybe we've strayed too far. Other times it seems that our circumstances in life, what others have done to us, may have turned us into sheep too blemished to keep. When years drag by, we wonder whether you will want to come and find us. O God, we want to be fit to be included. Please find us and keep us. Please heal us and teach us. Please convince us of your love. Through Jesus Christ. Amen.

Lev. 1:10; John 10:1–18; Matt. 18:12–14//Luke 15:3–7

17 O God, sometimes we do and say things that are so out of character that close friends exclaim, "What's got into you? You are not yourself today!" We say that we are "seized with fear" or "overcome by rage," so much so that it feels as though we were possessed, as though it is not we who act but some alien presence within us. But what would it be like to have no center, to be a legion of fighting self-fragments without any structure of command? How chaotic and crazy-making would it be to be taken over first by one and then another, to be terrible and

terrorizing, then craven and cowering, without any rhyme or reason! In our worst moments, we know the difference between our sanity and the mentally ill is only one of degree. O God, you ordered chaos at the world's beginning. Come, reassemble our shattered pieces. Reorganize us around the center that is yourself. Through Jesus Christ. Amen.

Matt. 8:28–34; Mark 5:1–20; 14:35–36; Rom. 7:15–25; Gal. 2:19–20

18 O God, sometimes we wake up in the morning leaden with heaviness, as if we would have to move Mount Everest to get out of bed. We manage to open our eyes and go through the motions. But our senses are dull and deadened, unable to perceive, much less enjoy, the goodness in the things that surround. Intellectually, we can rehearse the arguments about why this or that is worth doing, about why our lives are worth living. But we can't taste or see enough to keep believing it. O God, embrace us in our depression. Heal the pain that is killing us, and bring us back to life. Through Jesus Christ. Amen.

1 Sam 16:14–23; Ps. 139; Matt. 21:21–22; Luke 24:13–35; Rom. 8:28–39

19 O God, Bible stories tell how people only needed to touch the hem of Jesus' robe to be cured of what ailed them. But we know from experience that even a short encounter with the bigness of your goodness can turn our worlds inside out and upside down, can enable us to see ourselves and others with new eyes. O God, rend the veil from top to bottom. Banish the demons that possess us. Take up residence in our hearts and flood us with your healing power. Through Jesus Christ. Amen.

Matt. 9:18–26//Mark 5:25–34//Luke 8:40–56; Matt. 14:36//Mark 6:56

Sharing the Suffering

20 O God, sometimes we felt we would never get well, but you healed our bodies. Sometimes we seemed locked in our vices or paralyzed by pain, but you changed our hearts. Thank you for your love that transforms and your power that brings us back to life! Through Jesus Christ. Amen.

Matt. 9:1–8//Mark 2:1–12//Luke 5:17–26

21 O God, your healing presence is all around us. But we don't recognize it because we are looking for some flashy demonstration. Teach us to learn your ways of quiet discretion, to cleanse ourselves in silence, to immerse ourselves in music, to experience your touch in a friend's hug or listening ear, to experience your power in pills that the doctor prescribes. Through Jesus Christ. Amen.

2 Kgs. 5:1–19; Sir. 38:1–4, 6–10, 12–14

22 O God, we've all been sick in one way or another. Sometimes we have flu: we ache all over, our head is pounding, our throat is raw. Surgery leaves us too weak to move or fearful that any change of position will send out shooting pains. Horrid as these bouts are, we endure in the expectation of getting over it, of feeling healthy and strong again. O God, be with all those people who are never going to get better, whose present agony is the best they will ever feel. Make them to know the strength of your presence. Give them confidence that your love will hold them in life through death, and stay with them forever. Through Jesus Christ. Amen.

Job 6:1–13; Pss. 22; 31; 88; Isa. 25:6–9

23 O God, you know how hard it is to keep going when pain is our constant companion, when we can't be sure which hurts the most: to shift position or to hold still. You know how depression robs food of all its flavor, keeps us from tasting any goodness. You know how loss stabs and loneliness tears away our sense of worth. O God, wrap your compassion around everyone who suffers. Make us all know and feel the healing power of your love. Through Jesus Christ. Amen.

Job 6:1–7; Matt. 9:35–38

24 O God, there are so many people who wake up wondering whether this will be the day when they get driven out of house and home, when the relatives on whom they depend for support will be killed by terrorists or die of AIDS, when their own health will break irreparably, when they will lose their jobs and the possibility of finding any kind of work. Raise and torment our consciences until we do something effective to help them. Give them a share of your strength. Fill them with courage and hope to carry on. Through Jesus Christ. Amen.

Matt. 9:35–38; Luke 16:19–31

25 O God, in the Bible stories you heal people miraculously: the blind see; the lame walk; lepers are

cleansed; the mentally disturbed calm down, fall at Jesus' feet, clothed and in their right minds. Even now, some people get well contrary to expectation and beyond natural explanation. Yet when we pray, you do not *always* give us our health back in ways that we can recognize. The idea that you don't respond because our sins are many and our faith flimsy only makes us feel worse, fuels our fears that we aren't good enough, stirs our suspicions that you don't really care. O God, break through dark nights and tormented days. Touch us with your healing power. Convince us of your love. Through Jesus Christ. Amen.

Matt. 9:27–31, 35–37; 20:31–34; Luke 7:1–10; 13:10–17; John 4:46–54; 5:2–18; 9; 11; Matt. 8:14–17//Mark 1:29–34//Luke 4:38–41; Matt. 8:28–34//Mark 5:11–20//Luke 8:26–39; Matt. 9:1–8//Mark 2:1–12// Luke 5:17–26; Matt. 9:18–26//Mark 5:21–43//Luke 8:40–56; Matt. 11:2–6//Luke 7:18–35; Matt. 15:21–28//Mark 7:24–30; Matt. 17:14–21//Mark 9:14–29//Luke 9:37–42; Matt. 20:29–34//Mark 10:46–52//Luke 18:35–43; Acts 3:1–10

AIDS

26 O God, you made us dust-to-dust. We know that we will all die eventually. But AIDS is one of the worst ways to go. AIDS kills people before they die. People have to pretend not to have it if they want others to have anything to do with them. But the sham means that more people get infected. So AIDS makes people bearers of death to those they love the most. O God, forgive us for maintaining the stigma. Strengthen our wills and show us the ways to make AIDS drugs and human company available to the people we have been trying to ignore. Through Jesus Christ. Amen.

Isa. 52:13–53:12; Luke 17:11–19; Matt. 8:1–4//Mark 1:40–45//Luke 5:12–16

27 O God, the bodily pain would be bad enough. Mounting anxiety over the threat of death would be more than enough. But it gets worse when other people ostracize us because they're afraid they'll catch it . . . when society says we have the disease because we are bad . . . when women have to expose themselves and their children to avoid saying that their husbands are bad. O God, death is using fear and shame to claim more victims. Bring us to our senses. Free us to do what is necessary to preserve human lives. Through Jesus Christ. Amen.

Isa. 52:13–53:12; Luke 17:11–19; Matt. 8:1–4//Mark 1:40–45//Luke 5:12–16

28 O God, you must have been willing to make a world full of chemicals and let evolution take its course. Otherwise, why would the AIDS virus and its drug-resistant mutations have ever come into being? But you also inspired the minds of scientists to invent drugs that will keep HIV-infected people alive for decades. You have inspired volunteer doctors and nurses, teachers and relief workers to teach people how to use the medicines. Now we need one more big miracle of a kind in which you specialize. O God, break through the rocky surface, drill down to the sensitive tissue. Make us generous. Change our hearts! Through Jesus Christ. Amen.

Matt. 9:35–38; Matt. 8:1–4//Mark 1:40–45//Luke 5:12–16

Praying through Death and Dying

29 O God, you made us out of dust. But it's hard to believe that the people we love are just fancy mud pies. For years, we've known them as full of life and creativity, working towards goals, and polishing skills. We've experienced them as persons we connect with—giving and receiving and living so deeply into relationships that we scarcely know how to say who we are and what we're about without them. It's hard to accept that all of this—they and we—will unravel. O God, help us to trust you with our dead. Enable us to trust you with ourselves. Through Jesus Christ. Amen.

Gen. 2:4–7; 3:19; Job 14:1–14; 1 Cor. 15; Heb. 2:10–18

30 O God, our human lives are full of beginnings closed by endings and endings birthing new beginnings. Toddlerhood ends when we gain our stride. Early childhood ends when we enter school. The term ends when we begin our vacation. Undergraduate life ends when we leave the university for the last time and enter a new world. You might think we'd be so used to dying to the old and rising into the new that we'd have no trouble believing that the grave is just another door. The trouble is, we see people graduate and then see them off to job interviews in a business suit. But we don't see what comes next when we put bodies in coffins and bury them in the ground. O God, we have to trust you with this last transition. Fill us with faith to live as if the grave can't hold us. Convince us that we, like Jesus, will die but rise again. Amen.

1 Kgs. 17:17–24; John 11; 20:19–31; 1 Cor. 15; Heb. 2:10–18

31 O God, we want to believe that you will keep us alive after we die, that you will be good to us in ways beyond what we could ask or imagine, that you intend to include us in your peaceable kingdom that has no end. But animal instinct shouts louder. When we see the bodies of our friends or relatives nailed into a box and buried in the ground, it knocks the breath out of us. When the bus veers too close, when our competitor threatens our job, we don't have to think about it to be gripped by primal terror, by flight or fight, that automatically counts us and ours as everything, that stops at nothing to protect ourselves, to destroy theirs and them. O God, our faith is way too flimsy. We need you to do something to make your love and power more convincing than our fear. Amen.

Matt. 26:30–56//Mark 14:26–31//Luke 22:31–34, 39; Heb. 2:5–18

32 O God, in a way death seems banal—a humdrum, everyday feature of our world. Plants and bugs, mice and dogs, even other humans die all around us. Birth and growth, decline and death are the shape of biological life. In another way, our own death seems too outrageous to face at all. We are *not* simply dust to dust returning. We are persons, full of hopes and dreams and projects, lovers and beloved by many. How could you really love us and yet make us so temporary? O God, thank you for sharing our temporary life in Jesus. Strengthen us to face the hor-

ror of our own death and to enter into the wonder of resurrection life. Through Jesus Christ. Amen.

Gen. 2:4–7; 3:19; Ps. 90; Eccl. 3; Matt. 26:30–56// Mark 14:26–31//Luke 22:31–34, 39; Heb. 2:10–18

33 O God, we hate to admit it, but it's hard for us to tolerate ambiguity, especially when the stakes are really high. When the people we love best hover between life and death—with new medical technologies, days and weeks can become months and years—the tension becomes almost unbearable. We feel that we *should* want them to remain as long as possible, that we should cherish each remaining moment of our relationship with them. But each day becomes the torment of losing them while we have them, of trying to be present to someone who is already mostly not there. Traffic and bedpans and spoon-feeding, waiting by hospital beds for a flicker of recognition—these *are* tedious. But the truth is, watching is too painful. We want to run away from it. We get impatient for the plot to resolve so that we can get on with our lives. O God, give us the courage to be faithful. Give us the stamina to persevere to the end. Through Jesus Christ. Amen.

Job 2:11–13; Matt. 26:36–46//Mark 14:32–42

34 O God, St. Paul said, "To live is Christ, to die is gain." But for much of our lives, it is hard to feel that way. We are so invested in this world, in our relationships and projects, that we can't imagine life without them. But then our minds and bodies start to fail us, keep us from being the persons we were or contributing in the ways that we did. Pain or drugged wooziness become our choices. O God, be present now with all those who stand to gain by dying. Thank you for Jesus, who shares our agony and midwifes our death. Amen.

Job 3; 6:8–13; Phil. 1:19–26

35 Jesus, you know what it's like when the body lets you down, when energy drains, when you hurt all over, when your head is splitting and your limbs are aching, when your mouth is parched and your stomach heaving, when you can no longer think straight or pay attention. You know what it's like to feel terrible, and you also know what it's like to realize that you'll never feel healthy again. Jesus, reach down and bless the sick with your healing touch. Stretch out your arms to gather up the wretched. Reassure us that you are with us always, now and in the hour of our death. Amen.

Ps. 139; Matt. 27:33–49//Mark 15:22–39//Luke 23:32–49

36 O God, it really helps to make tangible connection. When someone dies, we keep her scarf or ring, his hammer or cane, not only because it helps us remember but because it feels like a way of staying in touch, of insisting that they are still real, of assuring ourselves that we haven't altogether lost them. O God, thank you for becoming concretely present in Jesus and in the sacraments. Thank you for all of the ways you assure us that we are not lost to you. Through Jesus Christ. Amen.

Matt. 1:23; 18:20; 28:9–10; 28:20; John 20:26–29

Sharing
Our Relationships

Friends and Enemies

37 O God, friendship is yours by nature. Thank you for giving us the gift of friends. Because they accept us as we are, they help us to be true to ourselves. Because they love us no matter what, we can afford to listen when they point out our faults. Because they know us so well, they can challenge us to stretch for what is beyond easy reach. O God, help us to be good friends. Thank you for being our best friend. Through Jesus Christ. Amen.

Gen. 18:16–30; Exod. 33:11; Deut. 34:10–12; John 15:1–17

38 O God, what we really want deep down is to be safe and to be loved. We want some people to know us for who we are, to appreciate and "cheerlead" our potential, to offer constructive correctives, to aid our attempts to achieve and to make a contribution. But very often, the wider world seems dangerous and hostile. Sometimes, people really are "out to get us." Sometimes, there are forces at work that seriously undermine us. Thank you for friends and partners, relatives and mentors who support us. Thank you for guaranteeing us a place in

your house, where we are sure to be loved forever. Through Jesus Christ. Amen.

1 Sam. 18:1–5, 19–20; 2 Sam 1:25–26; John 14:1–9

39 O God, when we go out on a limb, when we commit ourselves to controversial principles and to uncertain projects, it helps to have friends who become fellow travelers to urge us on. When we are the only ones heading in a certain direction, it's easy to worry, not merely that we might have got it wrong, but that our course is idiotic, that we are downright crazy. O God, thank you for friends who strengthen our resolve by sharing the risk. Thank you for adventuring with us, for running out ahead of us in Jesus Christ. Amen.

Eccl. 4:9–12; Matt. 28:18–20; Luke 22:28–31; John 15:1–17

40 O God, when someone close to us betrays us, it tears us apart. Underneath the hurt and anger, we feel radically unsafe that someone who knows us so well, someone we thought we knew so well, someone with whom we shared deep commitments and practical projects, could act in ways that threaten to destroy what we meant to do and be. Even when we manage to defend ourselves successfully, it's hard to feel that we're the winners, because we still feel connected. We didn't want victories that we couldn't share with them. O God, we pray for friends-turned-enemies. Assure us of your love, and teach us how to mend. Through Jesus Christ. Amen.

2 Sam. 18:5–19, 31–33; Ps. 55; John 13:2, 21–30; Matt. 26:14–17, 20–25, 47–56//Mark 14:10–11, 17–20, 43–50//Luke 22:3–6, 21–23, 47–53//John 6:70–71

41 Jesus, you told us to love our enemies as well as our friends. You have to know—because you had

enemies—that loving enemies is very hard to do. We have trouble even when the offenses are trifling. But it seems almost impossible to love the people who do us serious wrong. Jesus, maybe the best we can do right now is hold back from getting even. Maybe we can take one more step and ask you to love them as much as you love us. Hold us all in your loving-kindness. Work on us with your wily wisdom. Reconcile us with your healing power. Amen.

Luke 23:34; Matt. 5:43–48//Luke 6:27–28, 32–36; Acts 7:54–60; Rom. 12:14–21

42 O God, it's one thing to forgive our friends, people who really have goodwill towards us. But how can we afford to forgive our enemies, people who are out to put an end to things we hold dear, people who have actually attacked us or seriously hurt us? If we stopped holding grudges against them, we might forget what they're really like, let down our guard, and lay ourselves wide open for them to do it again. O God, convince us all the way down that you are our safety, that you are power to re-create and resurrect us, that your loving wisdom knows how to be good to all of us. O God, you are the ground that makes forgiveness possible. Root us more deeply in yourself. Through Jesus Christ. Amen.

Luke 23:34; Matt. 5:43–48//Luke 6:27–28,32–36; Acts 7:54–60; Rom. 12:14–21; 2 Cor. 5:16–21

43 O God, you are Perfect Love that casts out fear. If we could really believe in it all the way down, we would stop hating our enemies, hoarding the world's wealth, and thinking up desperate ways to get the better of one another. Help our unbelief. Enable us to forgive our enemies as you forgive us. Through Jesus Christ. Amen.

1 John 4:17–21

Households

44 O God, you are a Trinity of persons who live together in intimate relationship, each knowing the others deeply, each helping to make the others who they are. And you have set us in families to depend on one another, to give and receive from one another in countless exchanges. O God, thank you for enabling us to mean so much to one another. Thank you for families who build strength and generosity into one another's lives. Through Jesus Christ. Amen.

Gen. 1:26–28; 2:18–25; Eph. 5:21–6:9//Col. 3:18–25

45 O God, you made us to be born little, weak, and helpless; to be received into families who surround us with loving care, who rear us up through childhood, who stick with us through adolescence, who rejoice with us when we enter into our own, who in turn depend on us as they decline with age. O God, thank you for wholesome families and good childhoods. Thank you for the confidence that they breed, the hope that they foster, and the goodwill that they bring to life. Through Jesus Christ. Amen.

Eph. 6:1–4//Col. 3:20–21

46 O God, you are a welcomer of children. You even said that "childlike" is our best approach to you. We thank you for the gift of children who show us how to be open and curious and ready to learn. Through Jesus Christ. Amen.

Matt. 18:1–6; Matt. 19:13–15//Mark 10:13–16//Luke 18:15–17

47 O God, some people have a natural gift for parenting. They can hardly wait to have children of their

own: to cater to their needs; to awaken their abilities to focus and stare, to grasp and grab, to smile and babble, to crawl and to walk. They want to help little ones to grow and learn and become all they can. But the biology doesn't cooperate. They try unsuccessfully to conceive, or the pregnancies don't hold. They spend huge sums, subject themselves to invasive technologies, and still no baby comes. The aching void begins to swallow everything. O God, enfold and comfort couples with reproductive difficulties. Open ways for them to work with you to create new life. Through Jesus Christ. Amen.

Gen. 18:9–15; Judg. 13:2–25; 1 Sam. 1:1–2:11; Luke 1:5–25

48 O God, sometimes parents find their children different enough to wonder who they are and where they came from. Mom and dad watch and listen and try to coax communication. But they come up against stone walls of silence, iron curtains of incomprehension. They want to love and help, but they find themselves at a loss. O God, send your Spirit as a go-between to overcome alienation. Loosen tongues and unstop ears to hear and understand. Through Jesus Christ. Amen.

Mark 3:31–35; Luke 2:41–52

49 O God, you set us in families for mutual nurture, but all too often it doesn't work out. Mothers and fathers are crushed by the responsibility to give what they never received, to teach what they never learned, to foster what they do not understand. Living in close quarters makes us easy prey for one another, so that hurtfulness and indifference cut to the heart. O God, make your presence felt in abusive families. Enter each household with your healing love and transforming power. Through Jesus Christ. Amen.

Eph. 6:1–4//Col. 3:20–21

50 O God, you are eternal but you made us mortal, with a time to live and a time to die. Death tears the fabric of families, separating parents from children, grandparents from children's children. Death and disease, war and famine are no respecters of persons. Divorce and separation are not always timely. O God, strengthen single parents trying to love and support their children. Give young AIDS orphans resourcefulness to rear their siblings. Show us how to support them and to give them a better chance. Through Jesus Christ. Amen.

Ruth 1:1–5; Matt. 19:1–12//Mark 10:2–13

51 O God, down through the centuries, you have called human beings in many sorts of households—from polygamous Abraham and Jacob and David to monogamous Peter to people without partners like Jeremiah and Paul. Even now, you call some of us into marriage and parenthood, others into religious communities, some into the single life, and others into partnerships that cannot yet be blessed by the church. Help us to live into these different callings with Christ as our center. Enable us through faithfulness and hospitality and friendship to show your love to a broken and suffering world. Through Jesus Christ. Amen.

Jer. 16:1–4; Matt. 19:3–12; 1 Cor. 7:1–17

52 O God, help all those who struggle to make a way out of no way: wily mothers in Darfur, standing up to roaming gangsters who behead their children and steal their cows; almost teenagers in Africa, dropping out of school, scratching for food and shelter, providing for brothers and sisters when both parents died of AIDS; battered spouses hiding to protect their children; homeless people who find no room in the inn, who have given up society as a lost cause. Convince them that you are with

them wherever they go, often hiding behind the scenes, sometimes peeking out between the curtains, working with them to make a way out of no way at all! Amen.

Gen. 28:15; Matt. 1:23; 18:20; 28:20; John 2:1–12

53 O God, good families must rank high on the list of what makes life really worthwhile. Even a somewhat neurotic family can make all the difference. A family is like our ark against chaos, that keeps us on board through all weathers, stormy and fair. Normally, we expect that some of us will die, leaving others to carry on. But when too many are taken at once, it feels like the ship is breaking up and about to sink. O God, protect children whose families have been eaten up by disease; protect grandparents and children's children whose working family members have been killed in wars. Make us resourceful to provide their needs. Give them courage and open doors. Show them new ways to carry on. Through Jesus Christ. Amen.

Ruth 1:1–14; Job 1:18–19; 22:9; Ps. 68:5; Isa. 9:1; 10:1–2; Lam. 5:3; Jas. 1:25

54 O God, the Ten Commandments say to honor father and mother. How glad we are for parents who deserve it: mothers and fathers who surround their children with love, then build in discipline to train them up to wholesome relationships and fruitful lines of work. The gifts such parents give are priceless. Put into practice, their virtues are what enable human life to be a good thing. But what about parents who don't know how to do it because they had terrible childhoods, parents who "act out" on their children all of the mean things that were done to them? What about the tormented children who wonder what they've done to deserve this, who remain confused for decades about whether they were meant to live or to

die? O God, so many families aren't able to honor one another. Honor them with your presence. Pour your healing love into the wounds of the battered and the bullied. Assure them that you want them to survive. Through Jesus Christ. Amen.

Exod. 20:12; Deut. 27:16; Matt. 10:35; Matt. 15:3–7//Mark 7:9–13; Eph. 6:1–4//Col. 3:20–21

Confessing Our Failures

55 O God, today's world problems seem of mind-boggling complexity. And yet, the more things change, the more they stay the same. We can't afford to care about everybody, because there isn't enough to go around. We have to grab for power, because otherwise we may be squeezed out. We have to stand on ceremony, because we know we're no better than the people we put down. We have to strut our stuff to convince others not to call our bluff. O God, this is the way we behave at every level, and there is no health in us. Forgive the way we are ruining our planet, our nations, our institutions, our very selves. Turn our hearts. Help us begin again. Through Jesus Christ. Amen.

1 Kgs. 21:1–26; Amos 2:6–8; 6:4–7; 8:4–6; Mic. 2:1–3; 3:1–3; 6:8–16

56 O God, sometimes we know something is wrong, but we go ahead and deliberately do it anyway. Our motives are strong. We really want to do it—out of greed, out of demand for competitive advantage, out of hurt or fear or desire for revenge. Then we get on with our lives. We put our misdeed behind us, even become a different sort of person. But later what we did catches up with us in ways that we could never have predicted, gives

us a taste of our own medicine, makes us squirm with the realization of just how bad it was. O God, thank you for the ways life forces us to recognize and reckon with our sins. Thank you for chances to "come clean" with ourselves and with you. Through Jesus Christ. Amen.

Gen. 42–45, esp. 44:14–34; 2 Sam. 11–12

57 O God, you know how little there is to us. We fail so often to be true to the people and causes we care about the most. We risk intimacy and commitment, but that makes us hypersensitive to rejection and slights. When the wound digs deep we betray our loves. Other times fear makes us panic and desert the posts we had vowed to defend with our lives. O God, forgive our flimsiness. Work within us and alongside us to enable us to be true. Through Jesus Christ. Amen.

John 13:37–38; Matt. 26:14–16//Mark 14:10–11//Luke 22:3–6; Matt. 26:33–35//Mark 14:29–31//Luke 22:31–34; Matt. 26:58, 69–75//Mark 14:53, 66–72//Luke 22:54–62//John 18:15–27

58 O God, you shook the earth and blotted out the sun when your Son was crucified. How can you stand to watch us destroy and be destroyed? We do not know how to live in peace and harmony. We lack imagination to grasp how others see your world. Because we are afraid of what they will do to us, we try to do it first to them instead. O God, forgive us—singly and together—for doing terrible things to one another. Remold us, create your image in us once again, through Jesus Christ. Amen.

Matt. 27:45, 51; Mark 15:33; Luke 23:44

59 O God, we very much want to think of ourselves as worthwhile people. But we're so afraid that we're not that we can scarcely see straight. We teeter-

totter between covering up and exaggerating both what is bad and what is good. Help us to face the truth about ourselves and readily accept your correction. Through Jesus Christ. Amen.

Matt. 6:1–18, 23; Luke 18:9–14; 1 John 1:5–10

60 O God, we sing it out every Sunday, we say it in the creed: "We believe that you will come to be our judge!" Religious books encourage us to imagine high-court scenes with wigged judges, verdicts of condemnation, and hellish sentences. O God, we know, and you know, how easy it is for us to fail. Thank you for being for us, a Mother who corrects but shows us how and enables us to do better. Thank you for rearing us up to be friends and citizens of heaven. Through Jesus Christ. Amen.

Gen. 18:16–30; Exod. 33:11; Deut. 34:10–12; Isa. 66:10–14; Hos. 11:1–13; Matt. 25:31–46; John 15

61 O God, when scientists get confused, they get down to work and investigate. They try to come up with a theory that will put all the pieces together and enable us to see the world in fresh ways. But sometimes we'd just as soon not go for clarity: when a surprise pregnancy disrupts plans to finish college or return to the work force, when honesty and decency stand in the way of climbing the corporate ladder, when taking a stand for justice might cost us our reputation, when realism about global economics might deprive us of creature comforts. To tell the truth, we'd just as soon not face what we're really doing when we "act out" our self-interest. O God, forgive us for the terrible things we do in our confusion. Give us the courage to want to see things in your light. Through Jesus Christ. Amen.

Ps. 51:1–17; Isa. 7:10–16; 1 John 1:5–10

62 Forgive us, O God, for wanting others to stay bad so that we can appear good, and for competing for your love when there is more than enough to go around. Convince us that you can be good to our enemies without loving us the less. Make us so confident of your love for us that we become willing instruments of your love for our enemies, too. Through Jesus Christ. Amen.

Luke 18:9–14

63 O God, it's knee-jerk animal instinct to be competitive. What's the good of winning a race on the river if you can't make fun of the stragglers who rowed in last? What's the good of a summa or magna cum laude if it doesn't mean that we're better than the average students and those who don't pass at all? What's the good of membership in a club that's not restrictive? We're always scrambling for badges of honor because deep down we're worried that we're not worth anything. We're afraid that there isn't enough love to go around, that we won't get any unless we stand out. O God, convince us that your love is a given, that your power and good pleasure make all of our achievements possible, that you are the real prize! Through Jesus Christ. Amen.

Gen. 25:21–26; John 13:3–11; Matt. 20:25–28//Mark 10:42–45//Luke 22:25–27

64 O God, competition is almost as addictive as alcohol or gambling. We start small, but the stakes rise sky-high. Worse still, our focus moves off the real issue—providing good service, making an excellent business deal, uncovering new secrets of the universe, producing outstanding music, honoring the sport by playing so well—to winning, at least not losing face by being bested by somebody else. Sometimes we catch ourselves willing to do almost anything to win. O God, intervene to sober us up. Bring us to

our senses. Make us resolve to use our gifts responsibly, to advance our fields, to benefit others, and to offer something beautiful to you. Through Jesus Christ. Amen.

Gen. 25:21–26; 2 Tim. 4:6–8

65 Jesus, you were right about anger. Sometimes what other people do makes us furious. Sometimes what they say is so hurtful that we want to cut them down to size. We call them insulting names to turn them into nonpersons, so that we won't have to take them seriously, so that we can continue to believe that their feelings and interests aren't worth considering. O God, forgive us for the ways we try to erase each other. Help us to realize how you take each of us seriously by being with us all of the time! Amen.

Matt. 1:23; 5:21–26; 18:20; 28:20; Eph. 4:26–27; Jas. 1:19

66 O God, it's no wonder the Bible warns us about anger. It's like fire in the belly, threatening to spew out volcanically, to scald, melt, and burn everything in sight. Sometimes we'd like to empty it out once and for all so that we'd be finally free of it. Or we try to bury it down so deep that we'll never feel it. We fear its destructive power on others and on ourselves. But anger can be a good thing: it can alert us to injustice and danger. O God, teach us how to channel our anger for your purposes. Train us up to appropriate self-control. Through Jesus Christ. Amen.

Matt. 5:21–26; Jas. 1:19; Eph. 4:26–27

67 O God, we human beings know how to fight "dirty." It's not just that we use our minds to design "high-tech" weapons more powerful and destructive than animal teeth and claws. We fight with words. We know

how to tear people down with innuendo, how to fine-shred reputations with irony so subtle they don't notice until the damage is irreversible. We know how to fire shots that graze the surface, and we know how to deliver thrusts that cut to the heart. We can do it with smiles on our faces, all the while reassuring our victims that we are their friends. O God, forgive our devastating use of language. Wash out our mouths with the soap of your truth. Cleanse our hearts with the fire of your love. Through Jesus Christ. Amen.

Ps. 39:1–3; Eph. 4:29; Jas. 3:1–12

68 O God, you are Truth itself. Lies and deception are too unreal to stand a chance up against you. But often it doesn't seem that way to us. How many times a day will twisting the facts, using a little exaggeration or distortion, win the argument, make us members of the club, ingratiate us with those who want to believe and want others to believe what's false? We have to admit that there are many truths we don't want to know, don't want others to tell, don't want to face and deal with. We are afraid to live in the real world and to be the real people you created us to be. O God, forgive our foolishness. Discipline our equivocation. Stir us up to love Truth wholeheartedly, because that's the only way really to love you. Through Jesus Christ. Amen.

Exod. 20:16; Deut. 10:20; Ps. 120; John 8:31–47; 14:6; 18:37–38; 1 John 1:5–10; 4:1–6; 2 John 1–4

69 O God, most of us don't really know what it's like to be hungry. If we fasted on Ash Wednesday or Good Friday or Yom Kippur, we might get a clue. Parents and grandparents may remember rationing, or the depression when food money ran out before the week was over and people were left to eat what they grew in the garden. What we do know is what it's like to have spare change in our pockets and cash cushions in our bank accounts. O

God, trouble us with compassion. Motivate us to help. Through Jesus Christ. Amen.

Matt. 25:31–46; Luke 6:20–26; 1 Cor. 16:1–4; 2 Cor. 9:1–15

70 O God, you are holy. The Bible says that if we want to be your people, we need to become more like you; we have to become holy, too. But you know, we come packaged with a mixture of good and bad habits. Some of our impulses are strong and pull in opposite directions. When we find ourselves in situations that are particularly threatening or frustrating, we struggle for self-mastery. We're embarrassed to admit how often we don't behave very much like you. Sometimes, it feels as if we are "all or nothing" people: either we clamp the lid on so tightly that we can't pry it loose, or emotions geyser forth to scald and splatter all around. O God, send your Spirit to help us get ourselves under control. Through Jesus Christ. Amen.

Lev. 19:1–2, 9–18; 1 Cor. 13; Gal. 5:16–26; 2 Tim. 1:6–7

71 O God, it's one thing to let go voluntarily. When we finish school or change jobs or break up with a partner, it's as if the markers on our compass are smudged. Even when we've chosen new challenges, even when we are confident of discovering new fixed points around which to reorient, we feel the pain of the loss, as if we're leaving a piece of ourselves behind. So also and all the more so when our centers have been smashed, violently taken away from us by death and disaster, weakness and betrayal. So also and all the more so when we haven't a clue how to put Humpty Dumpty back together again. O God, give us stamina to wait and optimism to expect your re-creative surprises. Through Jesus Christ. Amen.

Ruth 1:1–18; Job 1–2; Ps. 137; Jer. 29, 51; Matt. 2:16–18; Luke 24:13–35; Matt. 24:4–36//Mark 13:3–37//Luke 21:8–37; Matt. 26:1–27:66//Mark 14//Luke 22:1–23:55; Acts 9:1–22; 22:4–16; 26:9–18

Expressing Appreciation

72 Given who you are and what we are, O God, it is surprising that you should care about us at all, much less enjoy our worship and our praise. Yet, given who you are and what we are, we want to offer you our very best. We thank you for the worship of this house: for the musicians who make it so beautiful, for the custodians and ushers who keep it in order, and for all those who come here with faithful or expectant hearts. Amen.

Job 38–42; Pss. 8; 29; 84; 95; 98; 99; 148–150

73 O God, thank you for the worship of this place, for the beauty that greets eye and ear and transports us into your presence, that lifts us out of the ordinary and gives us space and time to think new thoughts, to greet fresh challenges, and to know ourselves anew. Let these moments of quiet discovery spur us into action. Let them fuel our determination to work for a world where everyone has such chances to grow into the knowledge and love of you. Through Jesus Christ. Amen.

Pss. 27; 84; 96; 122

74 O God, being human is a confusing assignment. You made us persons; you nudge and beckon us to seek you. But you made us animals full of instincts for self-preservation, with fear and anger readily triggered to make life together with you and others hard. O God, thank you for your commandments that train our wills and point our directions. Thank you for those saints who have befriended us, whose lifestyles show us what you have in mind. Through Jesus Christ. Amen.

Deut. 11:18–21, 26–28; Pss. 1; 119; Gal. 3:23–24

75 O God, it's scary to realize how fragile we are when we take a tumble, or are thrown around in a traffic accident, or get really sick, or require surgery. It's also scary when we bump into the enormity of your presence. Putting the two experiences together can be terrifying, because they convince us how easy it would be for you to "rub us out" like an ant. O God, thank you for loving us and our world, enough to make us in it. Thank you for taking an everlasting interest in it. Thank you for counting us among the important people in your life. Through Jesus Christ. Amen.

Gen. 12:1–3; 15:1–21; 17:1–4; 2 Sam. 7; Pss. 8; 29; 89:19–37; Luke 1:26–38

76 O God, you know how much we need good models and helpful feedback to learn. If we got a gold star no matter what we did, we wouldn't have much skill at distinguishing the hurtful from the healthful, the important from the trivial, the excellent from the mediocre and the bad. Thank you for mentors who know how to correct without crushing, to inspire without intimidating, to invite without compelling, to encourage without lying or nagging. Thank you for people who draw us out and grow us

up and enable us to become all we can be. Through Jesus Christ. Amen.

Prov. 9:1–6; Matt. 11:28–30; John 14:25–26

77 O God, it makes such a difference how and how well people are organized. The same individuals with the same gifts and talents can be stymied and defeated by passive aggression, or energized into productivity and propelled into creative tasks. Administrators are necessary to make our work possible. Good administrators are worth their weight in gold! O God, thank you for giving some the gift of administration. Fill them all with your wisdom. Ease their burdens, and lighten their loads. Through Jesus Christ. Amen.

Gen. 41; 50:19

78 O God, most of the time we try to cover up our weaknesses because we don't want to make obvious to others the best place to attack. But sometimes, when we're desperate, we do ask help from strangers who just happen to be around. Sometimes they come to our rescue in surprising ways, but we hurry on, almost ignoring and somehow taking for granted what they've done. O God, make up for our rudeness. Bless all those we've failed to thank. Make us ready to lend a hand to needy strangers along our way. Through Jesus Christ. Amen.

Luke 10:25–37; 17:11–19

79 O God, the whole idea that who we are and what we do might show others what you are like is mindboggling. Our hearts are too narrow to measure your mercy. Our wits are too dim to pierce the mystery of your providential plans. But you are a God who specializes in shaping unlikely materials into advertisements of your

power and goodness. O God, thank you for molding us, clay in your hands! Through Jesus Christ. Amen.

Isa. 52:7–10; Matt. 5:13–16; Gal. 5:1, 13–25

80 O God, it took centuries of trial and error to evolve democratic forms of government, where all adult citizens have a stake in the common good and a say in the direction of their lives. Thank you for our freedoms of thought and speech, for opportunities to get an education and choose a career, for the organization and infrastructures that undergird our daily lives, for resources and initiatives that make prosperity possible and give more and more people a chance. Thank you for the wisdom of the past that shaped our present. Give us the know-how and the determination to hand down to others what we have received. Through Jesus Christ. Amen.

Rom. 13:1–7

81 O God, we're glad our lives are divided up into weeks, months, and years; into terms and seasons. It helps to give our lives plot, to shape our stories into chapters with beginnings, middles, and ends. Sometimes, when we've hit a bad patch, it feels good just to draw a line under that effort and to start over. Help us to begin with hope, to persevere with diligence, and to remain open to your surprises. Through Jesus Christ. Amen.

Job 38:12–13; Ps. 74:15–16

82 O God, when we're feeling overwhelmed and stressed beyond our limits, there's nothing like a walk along the beach to calm us down. The obvious vastness of the ocean puts our problems into perspective. Somehow, it's reassuring to experience how the world is very, very big and we are very, very small. The white waves crashing in, the

waters running back, over and over, give us a sense of stability and make us feel that everything is happening within a sturdy frame. O God, thank you for the grandeur and order of nature that fills us with awe and reminds us of your power and loving care. Through Jesus Christ. Amen.

Job 8:8–11; Pss. 90; 119:89–91

For the Incarnation

83 O God, when life gets really difficult, we sometimes wonder where you are and why you aren't making it easier. You know how readily we feel abandoned, worry that you are hostile or really don't care. O God, thank you for reassuring us at Christmas that you are not aloof but ready to share our lives. Thank you for being with us in the good times. Thank you more for being with us in the worst times, when projects fail, when relationships shatter, when love is lost through betrayal or death. Thank you for being Emmanuel, with us always, no matter what. Through Jesus Christ. Amen.

Isa. 50:4–9; 63:7–9; Matt. 1:23; 1–2; 18:20; 28:20; Luke 1–2; John 1:1–18; Matt. 26–27//Mark 14–15//Luke 22–23//John 13; 18–19

84 O God, it makes such a difference to us that you cared enough to become one of us, that you took real flesh and real blood, that you were really born and that you really died. If you hadn't, it would be easy to feel that you were unfair, demanding more of us than you do of yourself. O God, thank you for sharing our pain, our doubts and anxieties. Thank you for not calling armies of angels to the rescue. Thank you for persevering to the end with us. Through Jesus Christ. Amen.

Matt. 26–27//Mark 14–15//Luke 22–23//John 13, 18–19; Phil. 2:5–11; Heb. 2:10–18; 12:18–29

85 O God, your Word wouldn't have become flesh at Christmas if being embodied persons were such a bad thing. But it's difficult to get the balance right. It's easy to overindulge in eating or drinking or even exercise. And it's easy to escape and try to pretend that we are ghostly like the angels. What's difficult is to bring the two together in harmony, to make flesh praise you and our bodies temples of the Holy Spirit. O God, thank you for becoming human in Jesus. Help us to become more like him. Amen.

Rom. 7:15–25; 1 Cor. 6:9–20; 7; Gal. 5; Eph. 4:17–32; Col. 3:1–17

86 O God, integrity and coherence are so important. Without organization, the world is just a heap of things; people are just a bunch of individuals bumping into one another in the same place; thoughts and images float dreamlike following one another in time but without logic; our lives are empty sequences of "one damn thing after another." O God, thank you for your Word, speaking order and meaning into things from eternity. Thank you for the Word made flesh dwelling in our midst and giving sense to our lives. Amen.

Gen. 1:1–2:3; John 1:1–18; Col. 3:15–20; Heb. 1:1–14

87 O God, the Bible says that you are our *heavenly* Father. The Bible emphasizes that your ways are higher than our ways. Philosophers say that you have to be something very different from us or there wouldn't be enough to you to create and sustain the world. When bad things happen and we can't feel your presence or hear your answer, it's easy to believe that you are too grand, too high and mighty to care about us. O God, thank you for becoming one of us in Jesus. Thank you for stooping down to our level, to feel our pain, to suffer our anxieties, and to taste our death. Amen.

Isa. 55:6–11; Matt. 6:25–33; Heb. 4:14–5:10

Work and Creativity

88 O God, you came to make the bland flavorful and to give spice to life. You came to reveal what is hidden and to show off the world in surprising colors. Work in us to bring to birth what is distinctive and original. Teach us how to midwife the best in those around us. Help us dare to be interesting. Through Jesus Christ. Amen.

Matt. 5:13//Mark 9:49–50//Luke 14:34–35

89 O God, you are the light that shines in all knowledge. Keep us curious to seek you, nimble to pursue you, delighted to find you, eager to embrace you, and always desirous for more of you when you prove too big to grasp. Through Jesus Christ. Amen.

Pss. 43:3; 119:105; Isa. 55:6–11; John 8:12

90 O God, thank you for minds to think, for the gift of wonder, for the itch of curiosity that urges us on and keeps us at it, that makes us willing to lose sleep and miss meals day after day, year after year, if only we can come to understand. Thank you for the discipline of method, for analytical precision and faithfulness to the facts. Thank you just as much for creativity that blurs boundaries, that cross-fertilizes, that turns received wisdom inside out and upside down. O God, make us faithful in teaching and learning and exploring. Keep us honest, always loving Truth more than self. Through Jesus Christ. Amen.

John 14:6, 16; 18:37–38

91 O God, it is a real privilege to engage in university study. Some people around the world who are just as smart as we are don't even get to learn to read and

write. Here we can choose from so many subjects. Here we can spend all day helping one another learn how to follow out a line of thought wherever it goes. As the work piles up and the pressure of exams and deadlines builds up, stir up the love of Truth that we had in the beginning, fuel us with stamina to persevere to the end. Through Jesus Christ. Amen.

John 8:31–32; 14:6, 16; 18:37–38

92 O God, it's tricky to succeed someone in a job. If our predecessor was greatly loved and in post for a long time, we're in for a season of unfavorable comparisons. If the individual was going strong but forced to stop by mandatory retirement, he or she may resent our taking over. We may feel sorry and frustrated because we have no way to "fix it." But it's far worse if the person left in disgrace, having done something really treacherous or shameful. People may want to forget, to put the past behind them. People may expect us to be the messiah who brings in the new age. And that's when we really start to worry. What if the task is too much for us? What if there is something about the job that will play on our weaknesses to bring out the worst in us, too? O God, you are the author of new beginnings. Come and help us to be re-creative! Give us all a fresh start! Through Jesus Christ. Amen.

Josh. 1:1–9; Acts 1:15–26

93 O God, you made material stuff to vibrate and ears to detect the sounds. Animal barks and howls turn noises into signals. Without knowing what they're doing, birds upgrade them into songs. But what cave dweller would have foreseen human inventiveness with musical instruments, the mathematics of composition, the manifold combinations, the intricate coordination in orchestras and

choirs! O God, thank you for the gift of music. Thank you for our church musicians—for their talents and discipline, for their hard work and perseverance, for their consistent and soaring performances that shower us in beauty and catapult us into an experience of you. Through Jesus Christ. Amen.

1 Chr. 15:16–24; 2 Chr. 5:12–13; Neh. 12:27–30

Responding
to God's Calling

94 O God, it's such an honor to be included among your coworkers that when you first invite us, it's hard to resist gasping, "You mean *us*? Why, yes, we'd be glad to join in!" But your original approach is usually open-ended. You don't give us much idea of what we're really in for, except of course that we'll be coming alongside you. Then when you do get down to specifics, we're often so revolted that we want to get out of the whole thing. O God, thank you for sticking with us even when we run away. Convince us of your goodwill and wisdom. Enable us to be faithful to you. Through Jesus Christ. Amen.

1 Sam. 3:1–20; 1 Kgs. 19:1–5; Matt. 9:9–13; Mark 2:13–17; 8:27–33; Luke 1:26–38; John 6:52–65; Matt. 19:16–30//Mark 10:17–31//Luke 18:18–30; Matt. 20:20–28//Mark 10:35–45//Luke 22:24–27; Matt. 26:56//Mark 14:50–52; Phil. 3:4b–14; 2 Tim. 4:6–8, 16–18

95 O God, your call is irrevocable. Your insistence on having us to work alongside you is so resourceful that when one door slams shut you open up another and find ways for us to walk through stone walls. Inspire the church with like imagination: give selectors eyes to see,

church leaders and canon-law makers the will to make room for your surprises. Through Jesus Christ. Amen.

Isa. 49:1–7; Rom. 11:29

96 O God, it's not as if you give us a straightforward job description or checklist so that we can be sure to accomplish what you want done. You expect us to pay concrete attention, to be constantly on the lookout for your cues: speak a word of comfort here, call down the Spirit's presence there, help the gathered group to perceive the situation through gospel eyes! O God, wake us up and keep us eager. Convince us that serving you is freedom! Through Jesus Christ. Amen.

Hab. 2:1–4; Matt. 24:36–25:13; 25:31–46; Luke 12:39–46

97 O God, it's so easy to get mired in family feuds and office politics, to spend energy nursing grudges, and to tax our imagination getting even for petty slights. Forgive us for wasting time and opportunities. Thank you for newspapers, radio, and television that confront us with the depths of others' terrible suffering. Thank you for breaking through to remind us that we were made for higher things. Through Jesus Christ. Amen.

Col. 3:1–17; 1 Tim. 2:1–7

98 O God, the more we consider what human beings are, the longer we struggle to be faithful, the better we know ourselves, the more amazing it seems that you should be interested in us. Why would you insist on working with us, on making God-with-us and us-with-God central to your plan? O God, we knew you to be a Creator who makes something out of nothing. Thank you for doing what is even more difficult: making the stuff of our lives

holy, making us shine with the radiance of yourself. Through Jesus Christ. Amen.

Lev. 19:1–2, 9–18; Isa. 52:7–10; Luke 6:20–31; John 7:37–39; Gal. 2:15–21; Eph. 1:11–23; 2 Thess. 1:1–4, 11–12; 1 Tim. 1:12–17

99 O God, we have to confess, we're ambivalent. When things threaten to go really badly, we think we want a miracle to patch up our worlds in ways we already recognize as good. But when things are going well, when we feel we've got everything under control, we don't want you messing up our house or confusing us with bigger facts. We know our worlds are too small, that they will become cramped and confining if we insist on living in them forever. But they're all we know, all we can see, and we're afraid to leave them behind. O God, you talked the blind man into believing. Turn your persuasive powers on us. Open our eyes to see, make us willing to enter your brave new world. Through Jesus Christ. Amen.

Isa. 7:10–16; Mark 16:1–8; Luke 24:13–35; John 9

100 O God, you called us to be disciples, and we want to help build up your kingdom. But we have so many different ideas about what it is you really want. Sometimes, it's so important to us to be right that we do violence to one another: we kill, deport, invade other countries, and infringe constitutional freedoms. Send your Spirit to teach us how to distinguish our culture from your kingdom. Help us to appreciate the blasphemy of justifying our violence in your name. Through Jesus Christ. Amen.

1 Kgs. 18:17–40; Luke 9:51–56; John 4:19–24; Matt. 26:3–5//Mark 14:1//Luke 22:1–2; Acts 9:1–30; 22:3–21; 26:9–18; Gal. 1:13–14

PART TWO
FAITH SEEKING UNDERSTANDING

Praying the Questions

101 O God, you know the history of religions. You know how tempting it is for religious insiders to be self-righteous and look down on unbelievers, only to find that something happens to make their own faith vanish. Help us to remember that faith is not our achievement, but a gift enabled by your presence. Help us to marvel at it and be grateful for it, wherever it is found. Through Jesus Christ. Amen.

Heb. 11

102 O God, you can do anything. But it's quite obvious that you don't always do all that you can. You didn't save those people from the Boxing Day tsunami or from hurricane Katrina. You didn't protect the villagers in Darfur from murderous bandits. You didn't prevent the AIDS virus from evolving, and you didn't keep Jesus from dying on a cross. O God, you can do anything, but we don't understand your policies. Meet us in our confusion. Convince us of your Goodness. Help us to believe that when we die, you will raise us up again. Through Jesus Christ. Amen.

Job passim; Pss. 6; 10; 11; 13; 22; 31; 37; 38; 44; 49; 60; 69:1–18; 73; Isa. 40:21–31; Heb. 10:19–39; 12

103 O God, we know that we are in your hands. Whether we live or whether we die, what happens to us is ultimately up to you. But on this side of the grave it often looks as if the way ahead requires us to compromise our principles, as if we have to "do deals" to avoid disaster. When we don't see you interrupting to rescue us, it can easily feel as if you have left us in the lurch. O God, take hold of us, convince us that you are our Rock. Give us the courage that comes from believing that you are for us, all the way down. Through Jesus Christ. Amen.

Job passim; Pss. 6; 10; 11; 13; 22; 31; 37; 38; 44; 60; 69:1–18; 73; Matt. 10:24–33; Heb. 10:19–39; 12

104 O God, a lot of Bible stories show us how "hurry up and wait" is the story of your people's lives! When you call, we are supposed to commit ourselves *immediately*. But when it comes to delivering on your promises or bailing us out of trouble, you take your own sweet time! It's one thing to wait through business-as-usual seasons, when our worlds are running smoothly, when the cost is merely boredom with the tedium, a little stagnation for want of fresh challenges. It's quite another when dangers are real and present: when the enemy is overrunning our villages, slaughtering men, women, and children; when streets flood to the rooftops, when the boat is swamped with water and we're about to drown; when treachery smears our reputation and costs us our job; when the cancer is gobbling through our bodies; when the death sentence is about to be carried out. O God, you expect us to keep trusting even *while* the worst is already happening. Give us a mustard seed of faith in your resurrection power! Through Jesus Christ. Amen.

Gen. 12:1–4; 13:14–17; 15:1–21; 21:1–7; 22; Pss. 10; 22; 31; 38; 44; Matt. 24:9–14; Matt. 26–27//Mark 14–15//Luke 22–23//John 13; 18–19

105 O God, the suffering in our world seems chaotic. True, sometimes we behave foolishly and reap the consequences. But so much of the time terrible things happen to people without any apparent rhyme or reason, through no fault of their own. Yet even when we sink into the mire and see no prospect of pulling ourselves out, even when we are confused about where and whether you are, we feel the urge to protest, to demand, to act as if we expect vindication. O God, is that you really present with us in Sheol? Is that you already stirring in us with resurrection power? Through Jesus Christ. Amen.

Job passim; Pss. 73; 139; Matt. 5:45; Luke 13:1–7; John 9:1–3

106 O God, sometimes we feel so ashamed of who we are we wish we could disappear. We feel that the next best solution is to cover up so that no one will be able to see, so that we won't have to face up to who we really are. Other times, when terrible things happen and you don't seem to be doing anything about them, we feel ashamed to know you, compelled to make excuses for you by blaming the victims or telling other lies. We cover up our sense of bewilderment and betrayal for fear of what others will say and of what you will do. O God, convince us of your goodwill and understanding. Make us feel safe enough to face ourselves and to bring the horrors of human suffering out in the open with you. Through Jesus Christ. Amen.

Job 4–5; 8; 11; 42:7; Luke 13:1–5

107 O God, Augustine said that you made us for yourself, that "our hearts are restless til they rest in you." But you also made us in a world in which your presence is less than obvious. You made us weak and vulnerable to evils of many kinds. Even in a rich and peaceful

society, bad things happen that knock us off balance, that set us wondering whether life can be worth living and what it all means—things that make us question where you are and what you are doing and whether you really care. O God, we are restless. Break through locked doors, touch your wounds to our hearts, enable us to believe! Through Jesus Christ. Amen.

Job passim; John 20:26–29

108 O God, your power has no limits. Nothing escapes your understanding. Exasperated prophets sometimes say so in the spirit of threat to signal your amazing power to destroy. But more often, you reveal yourself to reassure us. If you contained chaos to create the heavens and the earth, if you are bigger than our worst enemies, if you know how to calm the storm that sometimes rages inside us, then we have nothing to fear. O God, convince us of your strength and wisdom. Coax us into entrusting ourselves to your love. Through Jesus Christ. Amen.

Job 38–42; Isa. 40–41:4; 43:1–44:8; 61–62:5

109 O God, the world we live in is such a mixture. Many things hint and wink at your glory—soaring music, elegant buildings, intellectual breakthroughs, a lover's touch, wintry trees bursting into flower. Sometimes we even feel your presence more directly. But other times you seem far away, absentee, even nonexistent. Often virulent evil seems to be really present instead. O God, we are only human beings. We don't know how to put the puzzle's pieces together. Please don't desert us in our doubts and fears. Put your finger in our wounds. Place your hand in our side. Mend our hearts. Restore our believing. Through Jesus Christ. Amen.

Pss. 10; 22; 31; 35; 38; 44; Luke 24:13–35; John 20:26–29; Matt. 27:46//Mark 15:34

110 O God, it's really confusing. Sometimes the Bible talks as if we are free agents, as if we are the ones who take the initiative in what we do and how we respond to you. Other stories imply that our hearts are more within your power than our own. But when a child loves its mother, who has the initiative? Which is it—controlling or enabling—when a mother loves the child into being someone who can love her back? How free is the child when it hates or rebels against abusive parents? O God, please don't hate us into hard-heartedness. Please love us into people who can love you back. Through Jesus Christ. Amen.

Exod. 7:1–7, 13, 22; 8:15, 19, 32; 9:7, 12, 35; 10:20, 27; 14:4; Josh. 24:1–28; Ezek. 18; 36:22–32; Rom. 7:7–25

111 O God, it makes all the difference whether you're for us or against us. So long as we fear that your final verdict on us is "no," there is a pocket of despair that saps our courage, erodes our stamina, makes us feel defeated before we start. But when we are convinced at bottom that you are for us, we can keep on trying to be constructive through a lot more frustration. Even the cross is bearable if it doesn't mean that you hate us. O God, thank you for your "Yes" to us in Jesus Christ. Amen.

Num. 6:22–27; Mal. 1:2–5//Rom. 9:13; Rom. 8:31–39; 2 Cor. 1:17–20

112 O God, your really present goodness can be very convincing. Sometimes when we've tasted or seen it, we know you're the one thing needful; you're what we've always wanted. The bigness of your goodness dwarfs our worst suffering enough to make us believe, even when we don't understand, that—despite all that's happened—everything will be all right. The cross of Jesus convinces us that you know what sorts of things have been happening and that you appreciate the price we pay to be part of your world. O God, keep on persuading us, until

we can say "yes" to you without any "ifs," "ands," or "buts." Through Jesus Christ. Amen.

Isa. 6:1–8; Matt. 17:1–8//Mark 9:2–8//Luke 9:28–36; Matt. 27:33–49//Mark 15:22–39//Luke 23:32–49

113 O God, sometimes the super-good really happens, something we wish for with all of our hearts but know to be impossible in the normal course of things. When the too-good-to-be-true happens anyway, we are stunned, then dizzy with joy as our world turns upside down and backwards. But then fear sets in. We don't tell anyone because people would think we're crazy. If we spoke it out loud, we would give ourselves away as believers in a new world order and open ourselves to its uncertain demands. O God, give us courage not to tame down the super-good into "nothing out of the ordinary." Make us bold to dare its promise with you. Through Jesus Christ. Amen.

Matt. 1–2; 28; Mark 16; Luke 1–2; 5:1–11; 24; John 1:1–18; 20–21; miracle stories generally

114 O God, you know all about geometry. Even we learned in school how the shortest distance between two points is a straight line. But life isn't like that. We start off in one direction and find ourselves sidetracked from one detour to another. We meet many interesting people, face many dangers, and get involved in fascinating projects that we could never have imagined in advance. Usually, we never get exactly where we thought we were going, although there may be metaphors and reflections of what we had in mind. O God, is this because your ways are higher than our ways? Is this because the journey is home, because we always travel with you? Through Jesus Christ. Amen.

Gen. 12:1–4; 27:41–45; 28:10–17; Isa. 55:6–11; John 21:15–25; Acts 9:1–30; 22:4–16; 26:9–18; Gal. 1:13–17

115 O God, the Bible stories don't try to hide it. You are the God of the near miss. Sometimes, you rescue your people by the skin of their teeth. Other times, you wait until the worst has already happened, until it's already too late. O God, you know that you can do anything, and we mostly believe it. But this sort of adventure is hard on our nerves. Make your power and resourcefulness vivid to us. Remind us of all the times we've seen you save us in the past. Through Jesus Christ. Amen.

Exod. 14:10–15:1; Ezek. 37:1–14; John 11; Matt. 28//Mark 16//Luke 24//John 20–21

116 O God, the Bible tells us to worship you in spirit and to crucify the flesh with all of its desires. Does that really mean that what our senses perceive and delight in has nothing to do with you? Why can't the taste of a ripe strawberry image your through-and-through goodness? Why can't fine chocolate intimate the sharpness of your sweetness? Why shouldn't the balance of a French sauce remind us of your exquisite subtlety? Was the runner really wrong to feel your pleasure when the body moves with grace and power? O God, you created us with bodies. Thank you for letting us use them to enjoy something about yourself. Through Jesus Christ. Amen.

John 4:20–24; Gal. 5:16–25

117 O God, you made us embodied persons. But you should be able to understand why, in our experience, this isn't obviously a good idea. Identifying with our bodies turns our bodies into symbols, outward and visible signs of our persons. Beautiful bodies are presumed to belong to attractive people, while defective bodies advertise their owners as personally sub par. Gang-raped women get cast aside as socially worthless just because their bodies are "damaged goods." These reactions are

deep-seated and instinctive and almost impossible for us to unlearn completely. O God, what were you thinking? Isn't it bad enough that bodily damage impairs our physical functions? Why does it also get to impose such heavy burdens on our self-esteem? Through Jesus Christ. Amen.

Lev. 22:18–24; Deut. 23:1–2; 2 Sam. 5:8; Isa. 29:18–19; 35:5–6; 52:13–53:3; 61:1; Mic. 4:6–7; Matt. 11:2–19//Luke 7:18–33; 16:16

118 O God, we spend much of our lives pulling our personalities into focus, becoming people who can make and keep commitments, who are apt to enrich and to undermine others in distinctive ways. But when memories dramatically fade, when Alzheimer's sets in, where does the person go? Is the person still present but trapped in a body she or he can no longer use to communicate? Has the person gone dormant? Does he or she slip away intermittently? Or does the person just not exist any more? O God, will you awaken us, or will you have to re-create us out of nothing when we rise again? Through Jesus Christ. Amen.

Ps. 139

119 O God, our bodies seduce us into partnership. In the beginning, we had to learn to recognize those waving and wiggling things as *our* hands and feet, given to us to move on purpose. How quickly we gave into the idea that we were a team, such a tight partnership as admits of no distinction. Not our bodies, but *we* learned to walk and talk, to sing and dance, to carve a turkey or sculpt a statue. *We* felt full or famished, exhilarated or exhausted. *We* befriended and loved, looked daggers and hated. But what about when major body parts quit working, when cancer gobbles up the good cells, when cataracts and deafness cut us off from human company? When the doctor pronounces the fatal diagnosis, it feels like the

whole thing was entrapment and betrayal. O God, why are we such easy prey? Is that the way you made us? Where did we go wrong? Amen.

Eccl. 3

120 O God, anyone over the age of thirty knows that the resurrection body needs to be different. Certainly, you know the aches and pains, the breaks and breakdowns we experience. You know that the bodies we have now were not made to last. But in a way, our bodies are part and parcel of who we are. We might like to be better built and have a more attractive nose or hair color, but how could anything very different in shape or size be us? O God, resurrection is hard to think about. It's scary and mysterious. Help us to trust you enough to find it wonderful and exciting, too. Through Jesus Christ. Amen.

Eccl. 3; Luke 24:13–43; John 20:11–31; 1 Cor. 15:35–50

Praying the Bible

121 O God, sometimes what we strongly feel seems out of synch with what the Bible says. We know our desires sometimes mislead us. That's why we look to the Bible and the church for guidance. But we also are convinced that some of the things we read in Bible stories just can't have got you right. Surely you didn't tell Joshua to slaughter all those foreigners just because they had a different religion! Surely you didn't approve of wartime rape and pillage! Surely it wasn't your idea to enslave the losers or the poor! But was it your idea for women to be silent in public? Do you oppose divorce and remarriage even in modern societies? Is it your idea that only heterosexuals should form households? O God, give us a double portion of Holy Spirit. Help us to discern our way through the Bible and the pronouncements of the church. Through Jesus Christ. Amen.

2 Tim. 3:14–4:5; 2 Pet. 1:20–21

122 O God, old-time mythology looks back to the good old days when people were bigger and stronger and smarter, with bodies built to last over nine hundred years. Modern science fiction looks forward to a future when lab technicians will produce superhumans by genetic manipulation. But you made us out of earth, earthy; clay that can't naturally hold its shape forever. Thank you for not coming as Superman but as fully human, mortal and vulnerable. Thank you for guaranteeing us eternal life in your hands. Through Jesus Christ. Amen.

Gen. 5

123 O God, by calling Abraham to leave home, you turned travel and migration into a spiritual adventure. Make our vacations times of rest and recreation, of shifting perspective and reconfigured commitments. Deepen us all in our awareness that we are rooted and grounded in you. Through Jesus Christ. Amen.

Gen. 12:1–9

124 O God, we love to read about Bible times when you were so familiar with chosen people. Abraham and Jacob wander around the region like other nomads. But, repeatedly, you break into their journeys with presence and promises. You show yourself to them to guide and to bless. O God, we need your company as much as they did. Interrupt and shape our everydayness. Make something of us. Be our friend, too. Through Jesus Christ. Amen.

Gen. 15; 17; 28:10–22; 32

125 O God, the story of Abraham shows us that even when we are as good as dead, when devastating disease, dramatic failure, uprooting, and lost relationships make us feel that our lives are over, that it's all pointless, that we just don't have what it takes to pull it together to try again, you are there laboring to rebirth us, to re-create us for imaginative projects, to thrust us into a

brave new world we never dreamed of. O God, you know that we are slow of heart to believe. Give us faith like Abraham. Convince us of your invigorating power. Through Jesus Christ. Amen.

Gen. 21:1–7

126 O God, Bible figures disagreed about whether you were in favor of child sacrifice. Your friend Abraham thought he heard you command it and understood your blessing to depend on it. But your prophet Jeremiah was sure of just the opposite: that whole burnt offerings of human children would be an abomination to you. Nowadays, some people still act as if they own their children, as if their children exist only to meet their needs. Some parents seize their daughters and sons as sexual partners. Others make their offspring targets of rage and frustration when they're afraid to pick on someone their own size. O God, forgive us for failing to protect abused children. Give us the determination and the wiliness to bring child sacrifice to an end. Through Jesus Christ. Amen.

Gen. 22; Jer. 7:30–34

127 O God, those Bible stories really understand how sibling rivalry breeds murderous jealousy. It's bad enough when authority figures play favorites. It's unbearable when the chosen strut and flaunt their privilege in our face. How unsurprising if Joseph's brothers wanted to kill him, even hurt their old father who had loved them less! Yet you meant it all for good. You were able to make Jacob's dysfunctional family a blessing to everyone. O God, cleanse our hearts. Make something good of our twisted lives as well. Through Jesus Christ. Amen.

Gen. 37

128   O God, as slapstick comedy, these plague stories are terrific. We resonate to the poetic justice of weaker lower-downs winning out over powerful higher-ups. We grin to hear how you made a laughingstock of Pharaoh and put the Egyptians to shame with bloody rivers and swarming flies, with punishing hail, devouring locusts, and hopping frogs. But as theology, how can they be true about you? Were you really just using the Egyptians, mocking them before you destroyed them? Don't you love everyone you made? If you hated the privileged and the powerful then, wouldn't that mean that you hate us now? O God, forgive us for making you in our own image. Open our eyes to see, stretch our hearts to feel the wideness of your love. Through Jesus Christ. Amen.

Exod. 7–11

129   O God, the Bible makes working for you sound like a scary proposition. Aaron's sons were struck dead immediately for breaking one liturgical rule. Saul lost his dynasty and was tormented by evil spirits because he wasn't genocidal enough in conquering neighboring cities. Judas couldn't live with himself after betraying Jesus, and the Gospels say it would have been better for him never to have been born. Yet Moses was a murderer; David was an adulterer; Paul persecuted Christians; Peter denied Jesus; and you still kept working with them. O God, we want to say "yes" to your call to us. Help us believe that you will be with us when we fall. Give us confidence that you will cause us to stand. Through Jesus Christ. Amen.

Lev. 10:1–7

130   O God, the Bible calls you "holy," which the dictionaries say means "separate." Why does it seem so logical that to see your face, to hear your voice, to

give and receive assurances, we have to withdraw from the ordinary, enter sacred spaces set apart, practice the art of meditation, shut down our conscious waking life to see visions and dream dreams? Maybe it's because you're too different to belong, too big to be contained by our worlds. Maybe it's because we're afraid and want to keep you locked in the tabernacle under quarantine. O God, thank you for breaking through our dimness and resistance with images to warn and call and comfort us. Thank you for barging into our worlds by speaking your Word in Jesus Christ. Amen.

Lev. 19:1–4

131 O God, in the Bible you are always full of promises. But between promise and fulfillment there always seems to be a "catch." In the Bible, you always delay to see whether your people will trust you to do the impossible. You put them to the test by leading them through entangling swamps and desert wastes. When their reward is in sight, you make them fight giants to get it. O God, to get your blessing, we have to really want it. Give us the clarity to want it more than anything. Give us the courage to risk everything to work with you. Through Jesus Christ. Amen.

Num. 13–14

132 O God, it's hard to see how you were fair to Moses. First, you drafted him into a job he didn't want. Then you used up his best years to govern the "stiff-necked" people you chose. And then you seem to blame him when they were just as rebellious as you knew they would be. After forty years of wilderness wandering, after all of that effort, surely Moses deserved to enter into the promised land! Or, did Moses enter into his reward along the way—when you showed him the backside of your glory,

when you met him in the tent of meeting and spoke with him friend to friend, when you made him as full a partner in your projects as possible, when you gave the trouble organizing the troops to conquer Canaanite cities into younger hands? O God, help us to throw ourselves into the roles that you have assigned us. Convince us that our real reward is working with you. Through Jesus Christ. Amen.

Num. 20:1–13

133 O God, we want to fall in with your purposes. We use our experience of you, what we learn about you from the Bible stories and other people's testimony, to try to identify what you would be for and what you would be against. We do our best, but it's confusing. Are you in favor of nuclear power, so that we won't burn more coal? Do you think the European Union is good because it builds positive ties and avoids wars, or will it wreck the environment with too many short-haul flights? Should we use our free tutorial position to build to strength, or should we spend it on the field that could use a boost in person power or reputation? O God, we're bound to get it wrong, like Balaam. Please work our mistakes into your plan. Through Jesus Christ. Amen.

Num. 22:1–35

134 O God, we can certainly be blinded by stubbornness. We can be so sure of our course and so task oriented that we barge "full steam" ahead without looking to the right or to the left. We are so determined not to listen to the people who really do know better that you sometimes have to get our attention by talking through an ass. O God, thank you for rescuing us with the ridiculous. Make us less headstrong. Give us the humility to pay attention to you. Through Jesus Christ. Amen.

Num. 22:1–35

135 O God, you make it sound so simple. "Choose life!" That's all there is to it! Our leaders say they meant to choose life for the people of Iraq. But look at the collateral damage! We mean to choose the good life for ourselves and for our children when we drive them to expensive schools in cars, when we feed them fresh fruits and vegetables shipped all the way from Kenya or Israel. Our intentions are good but our eco-footprint is large. We mean to choose life when we budget and buy cheaper clothes made by people on the other side of the world who work for slave wages. O God, we want to choose life, but we get confused. Give us the clarity of vision and strength of purpose to do it. Through Jesus Christ. Amen.

Deut. 30:15–20

136 O God, we are people of purpose. And we were not born yesterday. We know there are other people whose projects undermine what we most hope to be about. But sometimes it's hard to distinguish friends from enemies. Sometimes movements and ideas that could be our undoing disguise themselves as harmless or irrelevant. O God, we are limited. We have to choose our battles. Make us ready to turn to you for help in discernment. Keep us from sabotaging ourselves and betraying our commitments by making peace where we should fight. Through Jesus Christ. Amen.

Josh. 9:3–26

137 O God, we have pledged allegiance to you repeatedly: at baptism and confirmation, for that matter at morning prayer and evensong and Holy Communion, every time we say the creed. We want to center our lives around you and your purposes. We think we want to share your compassion for the poor and the powerless, the sick and the suffering, until we stop to realize:

your idea is not that we should send them scraps and left-overs and fleeting bits of our spare time. You call us to put their needs ahead of our own. O God, Joshua was right. We are repeat-offender covenant breakers. Don't just keep sending down your commandments. Enable us to obey them. Reach inside and change our hearts. Through Jesus Christ. Amen.

Josh. 24

138 O God, we have to confess, we have short memories. There have been times when you interrupted our everydayness with unmistakable Presence and unspeakable Beauty . . . other times when we marched right into a dead end and you opened a way out . . . still other times when we were smashed like Humpty Dumpty and you picked up the pieces. You'd think such experiences would be unforgettable. The trouble is, it's a strain to keep facing how little there is to us. Your manifestations are unpredictable. So we feel more comfortable pretending that we can do it all by ourselves, or relying on resources that look easier to control. O God, be patient with our foolishness. Keep on breaking in to mark us for life. Through Jesus Christ. Amen.

Judg. 2

139 O God, you know how we divide the labor. Men are supposed to strut their stuff in public places, to fight fearlessly and slaughter ruthlessly, to protect the kith and kin and bring the booty home. By contrast, women's work should be hidden, not less powerful, but therefore devious. The woman behind the great man stays behind so that he can stay out in front looking good. No wonder Barak made a fool of himself taking Deborah into battle. The story is still making fun of him, telling how Jael took his prize. The trouble is, these stereotypes put

everyone under too much pressure. Almost everyone is scared of violent conflict and disaster. Courage and cowardice aren't gender specific. Neither are wisdom and strategic skill. O God, help us look past gender clichés. Thank you for giving each of us the strengths we need to do what you are calling us to do. Through Jesus Christ. Amen.

Judg. 4–5

140 O God, we don't know exactly what ecstatic phenomena Saul and the prophets were participating in. But we have experienced your Spirit at work in our lives—midwifing creative connections, melting stonewall resistance, healing deep wounds we didn't know how to acknowledge, wearing away at us until we appreciate people we didn't at first like. O God, if some is good, more is better. Overcome our hesitations. Bring us into full collaboration. Let what we do and are together be as "catching" as fire! Through Jesus Christ. Amen.

1 Sam. 10:9–13

141 O God, there's a lot in the Bible that says pledges to you are unbreakable, that keeping our word to you is more important than anything else. That might make sense if we were wise enough to know what to promise. But we aren't. Jephthah vowed to sacrifice the first living thing he saw, and he went through with it, even though it turned out to be his daughter. Saul's men were faint with hunger and would have been easy prey. Priests and religious vow celibacy and then fall in love. O God, you know how to combine faithfulness with compassion. Keep us from being harsh in your name. Grow us up into the kind of loyalty you desire. Through Jesus Christ. Amen.

Judg. 11:30–40; 1 Sam. 14:24–46

142 O God, it's an old trick: maintain military dominance by keeping "rogue" groups from manufacturing weapons. For the Philistines, the operation was "low tech." All they had to do was to keep a monopoly on blacksmiths. Nowadays we want to keep North Korea or Iran or Pakistan out of the nuclear club. Back when, Philistines with swords knew how to do a lot of damage. But lobbing nuclear missiles as a power-politics gesture could repeat Hiroshima and Nagasaki, maybe permanently wreck our atmosphere, make planet earth uninhabitable by human beings. O God, maybe we're all rogue states, too childish to be trusted with weapons. Bring back the blacksmiths to beat swords into plowshares again. Through Jesus Christ. Amen.

1 Sam. 13:19–23

143 O God, sometimes we're angry enough to destroy things. Occasionally, the thought passes through our minds to wish others serious harm. But Christian education has taught us to repent of this. We learned that you want us to love our enemies. How can it be that you would punish us for not being cruel enough? Is slaughtering whole cities your idea of how to keep Israel from religious mistakes? O God, it is scary to read that you might be like that. Forgive us for crediting you with our limited imagination. Through Jesus Christ. Amen.

1 Sam. 15:1–23

144 O God, the Bible calls the woman at Endor a witch because the religious establishment wouldn't issue her a proper license for trafficking in spirits. But the story shows she had the gift, and she certainly wasn't wicked or mean. When King Saul came to her in desperation, she received him with compassion. She risked her life to conjure. She killed her fatted calf to honor your

image still shining through doomed human beings. O God, thank you for marginal ministers who care more about their calling than about power and recognition. Thank you for those who refuse to abandon the hopeless, for those whose persistent kindness relieves despair. Through Jesus Christ. Amen.

1 Sam. 28:3–25

145 O God, when you told David that his heirs would reign forever, he was thinking of his cedar house in Jerusalem, of expanding into Palestinian territory, of agricultural prosperity and mineral resources, of huge harems, fruitful and multiplying offspring as numerous as the stars. He never dreamed that you would become a member of his family. He wasn't hoping that his descendants would rule from a cross. He didn't expect his kingdom to last forever because you last forever, because a son of David is also the Creator and Governor of the heavens and the earth. O God, David must really have been surprised to discover what you had in mind. Will we be equally startled? Will we be able to recognize your plans made actual as the fulfillment of your promises to us? Through Jesus Christ. Amen.

2 Sam. 23:1–5

146 O God, idolatry seems to be one of the sins that you object to the most. But it's easy for us to pretend that idol worship is something people did way back when, something that modern people have left behind. We don't confuse you with figurines of wood or stone or plaster, which have eyes that don't see and ears that don't hear. We know you are Spirit and Truth. O God, open our eyes to see how we make gods of anything on which we feel our existence and well-being desperately depends, anything that we are convinced we couldn't live or flourish without.

O God, while there's still time, persuade us that you are the one thing we need, that you are the eternal-life giver, that you are love that never ends. Through Jesus Christ. Amen.

Isa. 44:9–20; Jer. 10:1–10

147 O God, we are so grateful that you don't hate foreigners. True, you called Israel to be your special people. True, when you decided to join the human race, you chose to be born from David's line. But it was too small a thing for you to save only one tribe or race or nation. O God, keep us always surprised and delighted that your goodness is boundless. Help us always to rejoice that there is more than enough of your love to go around. Through Jesus Christ. Amen.

Isa. 49:1–6

148 O God, you are the potter and we are the clay. It's good to know that someone of your skill is behind creation, even behind the movements of human history. Any newspaper or history book proves that we human aren't smart enough to shape events towards a wholesome result. It's good to know that you can reshape what gets distorted by our doings and misdoings. O God, please don't give up on us. You are the potter. Remold our hearts to love what you promise and to desire what you command. Through Jesus Christ. Amen.

Jer. 18:1–11

149 O God, you appear in our dreams and draw us to your service. Fill us with trust to risk, faithfulness to persevere, imagination to anticipate, strength to protect, and resourcefulness to nurture new life that is not our own. Through Jesus Christ. Amen.

Matt. 1:18–25; 2:13–15, 19–23

150 O God, none of those people in the story got more than glimmers. Magi-astrologers speak only of a king whose star has risen. Chief priests and scribes study the Scriptures to identify the place where the Messiah is to be born. All alike take the prophecies to foretell a worldly warrior mightier than the Maccabees, able not only to displace Herod but to overthrow Caesar's legions. They were not figuring on God-with-us, a preacher-teacher-healer who would stand down Satan, reign from the cross, and rise from the dead. O God, we also get glimmers. Help us—like the magi and Joseph—not to fear, but to welcome your appearing with readiness to act. Through Jesus Christ. Amen.

Matt. 2:1–12

151 Jesus, the Christmas Bible stories tell how your family fled to Egypt to escape Herod's pogrom. Even as an adult, you identified yourself with homeless wanderers who have no place to lay their heads. Be present now with all those who have been driven out of homes and villages, who flee for their lives only to arrive in places that don't want them, with people who are afraid of being overrun by them, who don't have or want to spend the money or take the trouble to help them get established enough to contribute to new communities as they build new lives. Convict us, who are relatively well off and safe, of our fear and greed, of our responsibility to assist and to welcome. Give our government and the world community wisdom and resolve to meet their needs. Amen.

Matt. 2:13–18

152 Jesus, you were certainly right about prophets being without honor in their own countries. Within the family, town, or village, we're supposed to be peers, each person just as good or worthy, just as entitled

to take up space and use communal resources as anyone else. When someone stands out, they show us up. We shared the same beginnings. We had the same chances. There must be something wrong with us; there must not be as much to us, or we would rise, too. *They* upset the social apple cart. *We* feel threatened. And so we try to restore equilibrium by cutting them down to size. Jesus, forgive us for trampling down your kingdom in our midst. Open our hearts to welcome your Spirit. Make us willing to become prophets, too. Amen.

Matt. 13:53–58

153 Jesus, you ask, Who do *we* say that you are? But we could reverse the question: Who do *you* say that we are? Open our hearts to your answers. You are our Creator. Our identities are bound up together. Make us glad that who we are has everything to do with you. Amen.

Matt. 16:13–20

154 O God, your prophecy of wars and rumors of wars seems to be coming true. How can we enforce peace with war? How can we establish peace among people who don't want peace? Send your Spirit to hover over all creation. Move in the hearts of all individuals and peoples. Convince us that *you* are our safety. Establish your peace on earth. Through Jesus Christ! Amen.

Matt. 24:3–8

155 O God, many of Matthew's stories make us fear that you are a hard master, imposing heavy burdens and threatening failures with outer darkness and weeping and gnashing of teeth. Jesus' warning that we must be perfect the way you are perfect could drive us to despair. O God, help us to remember that you are the One

who makes a lot out of a little, the One who multiplies loaves and fishes to feed the multitudes. Give us confidence to invest everything in your service. Take our one talent and turn us into five-talent people. Through Jesus Christ. Amen.

Matt. 25:14–30

156 O God, you were right: the poor are always with us. You knew we would be too afraid to give up grasping and grabbing, hoarding and accumulating much more than we need, more than we could ever consume. Having enough is a matter of life and death, so how can we afford to take chances? It's an old, old story: the rich get richer, the poor get poorer, til comes the revolution, which unfortunately only manages to reverse roles. O God, during and after the Second World War, when there were real shortages, we were willing to share so that everyone could have something. Revive our sense of community. Now that there is more and plenty, give us imagination to rethink the system. Make us willing to cut back our surplus so that everyone can have enough and to spare. Through Jesus Christ. Amen.

Matt. 26:6–13

157 O God, the parable says that agriculture is mysterious: the farmer plants the seed and weeds and hoes, and crops come up, but the farmer knows not how. Yet we have learned a lot about plant biology, about what is happening within and outside the seed before shoots appear above the ground. Biochemists study with precision how genes manage and sequence growth and development. They describe in detail what factors interrupt, abort the fruit, and make things go wrong. In fact, we understand it so well that we can crossbreed new strains deliberately, even reach in with tiny tools to mod-

ify the crops genetically. O God, knowledge is power, but we aren't wise enough to dominate. Save us from a cynical desire to manipulate. Let discovery instead stir wonder and humility before the Maker's hand. Through Jesus Christ. Amen.

Mark 4:26–29

158 O God, no matter how often you heal us, we are still half-blind to your Goodness. To see clearly how boundless it is, we would really have to let go of those other goods we use to define ourselves. To enter the brave new world of your kingdom, we would have to liquidate our substantial investments in the status quo. O God, thank you for bearing with us while we surrender gradually. Keep on creating crises that make us want more healing, here and now. Through Jesus Christ. Amen.

Mark 8:22–26

159 O God, it's not hard to see how beatitudes and woes would encourage the down and out. If we were in their place, we would enjoy dreaming of the day when we would live in a palace waited on by servants, while the well-heeled who ignored us had to sell magazines in the rain and sleep rough. But as things are, *we* are the ones who are rich and well-fed, with each day bringing new enjoyments. O God, do you really mean to count us out? Can we enter the kingdom of heaven with all of our wealth and privilege? What do you want *us* to do? Through Jesus Christ. Amen.

Luke 6:20–26

160 O God, where people are concerned, isn't it a little simplistic to speak of good trees bearing good fruit and bad trees producing bad? You know, we all

know, most of us are mixtures. Even saints have their weaknesses and failings. Even tyrants and Mafia bosses have their good points. Which of us is really pure in heart? Which of us is rotten to the core? O God, we have to admit that we have produced some fruit that we are ashamed of. Come to us as sun and rain. Enable us to bear good fruit, too. Through Jesus Christ. Amen.

Luke 6:43–45

161 O God, if we really believed in your welcome, we wouldn't be so afraid of getting rejected. If we weren't terrified of being left out, we wouldn't have to pretend to be so deserving. If we weren't trying so hard to prove ourselves, we wouldn't be constantly trying to make others look bad. O God, bring us to our senses. Convince us that there is always room for us at home. Through Jesus Christ. Amen.

Luke 15:11–end

162 O God, Herod was curious about Jesus. Herod was itching for the momentary thrill of a circus spectacular. He wanted a ringside seat on signs and wonders and miraculous stunts. He needed to confirm his suspicion that what we normally see isn't all we'll get. He wanted to titillate himself with your grandeur without paying the price of admission. O God, forgive us for flirting with discipleship. Strengthen us to follow wherever you go. Help us to live into your Reality by taking up our cross. Through Jesus Christ. Amen.

Luke 23:6–12

163 O God, that story about Pilate feels all too familiar. Part of him wanted to do the right thing, even went to some lengths to respect human dignity. But

another part wanted to keep his job, maintain his lifestyle, even try for promotion. When the political costs got too high, he gave in. We also wish everyone could have good food and housing and medical care. We want to quit stuffing people into squalid prisons. We don't want to be party to torturing suspects into false confessions or holding them indefinitely without trial. But we do only so much about it. We are afraid to go very far. O God, disturb us until we find our equivocation intolerable. Give us integrity like yours. Through Jesus Christ. Amen.

Luke 23:13–25

164 O God, what was your point in putting brutal torture at the center of our religion? Even if Jesus had to die for our sins, why couldn't he have passed away at home in bed at a ripe old age? Or drunk the hemlock like Socrates after a theological discussion with his friends? Were you trying to model how to be heroes? Or was it because your cross is an exposé? Were you trying to show us how our best intentions pave the way to hell? Were you trying to harrow hell by identifying with us in the worst that we could suffer, be, or do? O God, brutal torture is part of our present. Send Jesus to work with us to bring it to an end. Amen.

Luke 23:26–49

165 O God, when it came right down to it, public protest of your innocence was left to strangers. The disciples were afraid of being counted guilty by association. They were terrified that other crosses might be waiting for them. Perhaps at Calvary, where they watched from a distance, they were overcome with horror and grief. The centurion was close enough to see but detached enough safely to say what he recognized to be true. O God, there are many in our society with whose suffering

we are not personally connected. Pierce our consciences. Open our eyes to look. Make us bold to advocate for some of them. Through Jesus Christ. Amen.

Luke 23:47

166 O God, the dead bodies of those we love are important to us. Something in us wants to keep them with us as long as we can. Because the soul is gone, because there is nothing inside to hold the body together, people used to soak corpses in chemicals or pack them in spices and wind them with strips of cloth to help them keep their shape. Nowadays we do it intravenously, but undertakers can't really say how long the effect lasts. O God, we know you made us from dust to dust returning. But this is hard for us to face. And it's painful finally to let go. Through Jesus Christ. Amen.

Luke 23:50–56

167 O God, deep down we're always worried about whether the world will make room for us. We get the sense that it's really important to earn our place. Yesterday's achievements scarcely pay tomorrow's rent. So glory from one another is a kind of insurance policy: it means that others count us important enough not to throw out. The trouble is, the effort is exhausting. We won't be able to keep it up forever. O God, reassure us that you really want to include us. Bring us to the place that you have prepared. Through Jesus Christ. Amen.

John 5:44

168 O God, your Good-Shepherd image makes leadership seem straightforward. All the shepherd has to do is lead the sheep to food and water and to fight off wild beasts. It may be hard and risky work, but at

least the task is clear. Nowadays, states are failing because the people in power don't know how to create and maintain the infrastructures needed to deliver basic goods and services. Since they lack the skill to do what's needed, they reckon they might as well use their power to grab all they can. Swiss bank accounts swell, while ordinary people are at a loss. O God, you are the Good Shepherd. Water our leaders from the well of your wisdom. Pasture them on your goodwill. Through Jesus Christ. Amen.

John 10:1–18

169 O God, you know how often there is not enough to us to keep our promises when it really matters. Yet you call and are always recalling us into your circle of friends. Give us—like Peter—integrity to love you with all that we have and all that we are, humility to rely on your willing help, and courage to take up our cross and follow you. Through Jesus Christ. Amen.

John 21:15–23

170 Jesus, St. Paul saw you on the Damascus Road and allowed you to reform him from the inside out. He could describe love so well because he knew your love at work to make him a new creation. St. Paul says that when you met him, he was not patient and kind. His letters show that he remained a little irritable. His writings also prove you made him someone who could rejoice in right, bear hardship with hope, and praise you to the end. Jesus, you did it before, and you can do it again. Change our hearts, as soon as possible, right now! Amen.

Gal. 1:11–24

171 O God, St. Paul was right. If we had to earn your love by keeping laws and commandments,

our situation would be hopeless. But our prospects aren't much better if we have to believe before you'll love us instead. We need it to be the other way around: your favor comes first and turns us into the kind of people who want to please you, who can trust your promises and work alongside you. O God, thank you for taking the initiative. Love us into obedience. Give us the gift of faith. Through Jesus Christ. Amen.

Gal. 3:6–14

172 O God, "divide and conquer" may be difficult to do, but it's easy to understand. We could say "spirit is good and flesh is bad," and then we could deny the body its satisfactions and cut ourselves off from creature comforts and try to turn our minds to higher things. But maybe you made us personal animals with the hope that we would not amputate but learn to coordinate body and mind with the help of your Spirit. Maybe you wanted us to knead your light into our clay. O God, there's no easy recipe for how to do this. Thank you for your indwelling Spirit who teaches us. Thank you for coming among us to point the way. Through Jesus Christ. Amen.

Col. 2:20–3:4

173 O God, we've read the books about ancient culture. But that doesn't make St. Paul's attitude much easier to sympathize with. It's one thing to say he couldn't change Roman imperial policy. But if he really loved Onesimus, why didn't St. Paul ask his master to set him free? It's one thing to belong to you, our Creator. But you came to bring release to the captive. How could you approve of degrading a person into property bought and sold by merely human beings? O God, it's easy to criticize others. Wake us up to the ways our lifestyles abuse and

exploit. Sting us with repentance, and show us how to stop it. Through Jesus Christ. Amen.

Philemon (entire)

174 O God, the Bible says you know all about us—more than any parent or teacher, more than Freudian superegos, more than we know about our very own selves. This would be a scary thought if we had to think of you as an aloof, demanding authority figure. Happily, you are too big for that. Besides, you came among us in Jesus to experience what it's like to be human from the inside. Because you made our weaknesses your own, you can be trusted to show your almighty power in mercy and pity. Thank you for Jesus, our great high priest! Amen.

Heb. 4:14–16

175 O God, we don't need the book of Revelation to tell us not to tolerate people who disagree with us. That comes to us naturally! Especially where differences are sharp and arguments heated, we could almost enjoy the thought of your making our enemies sick or commanding us to exclude them from the fold. The trouble is, these reactions prove that *we* are not pure in heart. The depth of our division displays our fallibility. Teach our church how to combine discipline with humility. Send your Spirit to show us how you love your enemies. Show us how to love ours. Through Jesus Christ. Amen.

Rev. 2:18–28

PART THREE
CARING FOR GOD'S WORLD

Sharing the Terror

176 God of All Mercy, pour down your healing love on all those who were affected by the bombings in London: on those who were killed, on those who have been seriously disabled, on frantic and grieving friends and family, on bone-tired emergency workers and exhausted investigators, on doctors and nurses doing their best to help the wounded mend. Reveal yourself to them once more as resurrection and life. Through Jesus Christ. Amen.

Pss. 25:1; 46; 132:1; Lam. 3:19; 5:1; Matt. 24:15–22//Mark 13:14–20//Luke 21:20–28; 2 Cor. 1:3–7

177 O God, we know we couldn't be persons without memory. But when bad things happen, memory seems to be our enemy, because it makes us experience them again and again. Put your loving arms around all those train passengers and bus riders, passersby and emergency workers who saw and heard things they cannot yet say, things that come out in shudders and sobs, nightmares and depression. Let the strength of your presence calm their fears and order their minds. Through Jesus Christ. Amen.

Pss. 25:1; 46; 132:1; Lam. 3:19; 5:1; 2 Cor. 1:3–7

178 O God, it's hard to imagine the agony of bomb victims, whose limbs were blown off or whose skin was burned. Relieve their pain, give them the physical stamina they need to recover and the courage they need to hope for the future. Through Jesus Christ. Amen.

Job 7:1; Pss. 119:77, 156; Lam. 3:19; 5:1; 2 Cor. 1:3–7

179 O God, you promised to be present where two or three are gathered together. Even when we descend into the hell of human misery, you are there. Make hostages and prisoners know and feel that you are with them. Calm fears. Banish desperation. Open captors' eyes to recognize each victim as your own beloved child. Amen.

Job 7:1; Pss. 25:1; 46; 119:77, 156; 132:1; 139; Lam. 3:19; 5:1; Matt. 18:19–20

180 O God, we root into friends and family so deeply that any kind of separation pulls and tears at the fabric of who we are. Any kind of death might threaten to unravel us. But when our dearest ones are lost and we don't know whether they are dead or alive, we are left in limbo—dangling in suspended animation between hope and fear, between expectation and despair. We don't know how to react. We feel panicked and powerless because there's nothing we can do. O God, strengthen those who wait with your patience. Enfold them with your love, when the answer is too hard to bear. Through Jesus Christ. Amen.

Gen. 42:38; 44:18–34; Luke 15:11–32; 2 Cor. 1:3–7

181 O God, so long as suicide bombers were in some other part of the world, they could remain an abstraction. But now that they have struck in

London and New York, where some of us work and others of us vacation, they suddenly seem very concrete and real. Now we're afraid that we or those we love will get blown up, that our public-transportation-driven way of life will be disrupted. We're afraid of what has been happening to our society while we weren't noticing. Hold us all in your love, which is stronger than death. Through Jesus Christ. Amen.

Pss. 25:1; 132:1; Song 8:6

182 O God, arbitrary violence leaves us scared and bewildered. Boarding a bus or walking through a crowd, we are suspicious: anyone could be our enemy, especially if they look like the people we saw pictured in the paper or on TV. O God, keep us from jumping to conclusions. Forgive our ever-readiness to divide the world into "us" versus "them." Through Jesus Christ. Amen.

Ps. 22:12–13

183 O God, you know how fear and frustration make us ready to do anything, whether it will help or not. Big powers invade, bomb, and destroy other nations. Little powers are more old-fashioned, amputating with machetes and decapitating with knives. Only your love is strong enough to banish terror and tame our brutality. Comfort captives, convert oppressors, civilize us into your kingdom, where we can all be safe and secure. Through Jesus Christ our Lord. Amen.

1 John 4

184 O God, you know how animal fear turns to meanness. When we feel hurt or threatened, we want to give worse than we got, to get back. It's not enough to eliminate danger by killing. We want to torment

and degrade, to humiliate them before they die. O God, forgive us for trying to destroy your image in others. Forgive us also for the way we pervert your image in ourselves. Through Jesus Christ. Amen.

Ps. 109

185 O God, terror makes us hate, and hate makes us demonize our enemies. But even the newspapers tell how many terrorist bombers seemed outwardly unremarkable to their neighbors, young people trying to find their way, looking to others for inspiration and guidance. We don't know their inward thoughts and feelings, but help us to believe that they also are your children. Convince us how much you love each and all of us. Bring us to some measure of understanding, and enable us to forgive. Through Jesus Christ. Amen.

Luke 23:34; Matt. 5:38–48//Luke 6:23–36; Acts 7:60; Rom. 12:14–21

186 O God, what kind of world is this that adults are going to leave for their children? There is fighting everywhere, and they tell us we live in a time of peace. You are the only one who can help us. O God, give us a new world in which we can be happy, in which we can have friends and work together for a good future . . . a world with no more of the cruelty that tries to destroy us in so many ways. Amen.

Rev. 21–22

187 O God, even within our own families, we sometimes get so upset that we splatter our anger all over the room onto whomever happens to be around. But there are orders of magnitude. What would it be like to think it permissible, even a right and noble thing to blow up oneself and other human beings with bombs? O God, the

thought terrifies us, the reality so stuns us that we don't want even to try to understand this. Only your mind is wide enough to take this in. Only your heart is deep enough to love the perpetrators and be good to the victims. We need your wily wisdom to persuade us, to teach us how to live together in better ways. Through Jesus Christ. Amen.

Ps. 139

188 O God, we often *say*, because we'd like to *think*, that the terrorist bombings are senseless. But what if the bombers really see us as villains, as beneficiaries of a society that doesn't respect them, that doesn't give them choices that they find meaningful or the chance to make a middle-class living without giving up too much of what they prize? O God, we haven't begun to fathom the challenges of multicultural living. Give us all more imagination. Give our leaders wisdom to face tough truths. Keep us from rebuilding on the sand. Through Jesus Christ. Amen.

Hab. 2

189 O God, we have to confess that we don't summon strength to face the horror of human beings blown apart by bombs day after day. We can focus on it for a few minutes—long enough to read the news article or watch the TV spot—but even then we shift into lurid curiosity that pries to avoid being torn up with compassion that identifies. Bomb-blast survivors don't have that luxury. Explosions still replay in their dreams. Their bodies shudder at any loud noise. When they try to walk or run or reach, they remember they have lost their legs or arms. Enfold them in your love. Give us all the courage we need to accompany one another. Through Jesus Christ. Amen.

Pss. 25:1; 119:77, 156; 132:1; 137:6; Lam. 2:13; 3:19–24; 5:1

190 O God, thank you for all those who risk life and limb, heart and health to protect others. For police and firefighters, for ambulance and hospital workers, for passersby who lent a helping hand. Give them stamina for their work and healing from their own traumas at what they have faced and seen. Through Jesus Christ. Amen.

Matt. 10:42; 25:31–46; John 15:13

191 O God, we don't like to admit it, but our way of living depends on taking risks with other people's lives. Police place themselves in harm's way on a daily basis. And we put them in a position of split-second deciding about whether to kill someone else. When they make honest mistakes on our behalf, *they* still have to live with the memory of pulling the trigger or striking the blow. O God, thank you for their courage. Be their shield and safety. Show us how to protect ourselves without taking people's lives. Through Jesus Christ. Amen.

Matt. 10:42; 25:31–46; John 15:13

192 O God, you identified with the tortured when you died on the cross. You taught us that whatever we do to the least powerful, we do to you. Forgive all nations and organizations who participate in brutalizing and degrading human beings made in your image. Give leaders the will and the wisdom to set new policies and put them into effect. Strengthen commanding officers and soldiers who try to keep discipline while they themselves are in harm's way. Protect us all from the worst that is in us, from what our individual and collective fears can drive us to do. Amen.

Matt. 25:31–46; Matt. 27:32–54//Mark 15:21–39//Luke 23:26–49//John 19:17–30; Heb. 13:5

193 *[7/7]* O God, it's some years ago now, but—for thousands of people––the explosions still interrupt their sleep. For some, it's nightmares so vivid that they can feel the train lurch, the carriage rock, bodies flying in confusion; they wake up smelling the stench, gasping for breath through stifling heat, wishing but unable to let out screams to pierce the engulfing dark. For others, it's struggling to learn new ways of moving with wheelchairs and prosthetics, trying to recover old skills and learn new ones, just to become able to do some meaningful job. For still others, theirs is the aching void of the self they once were, of the significant other they once held, of colleagues and workers with whom they shared life. O God, you re-create and resurrect. You furnish more than sentimental comfort. Help all of the suffering to build new lives. Through Jesus Christ. Amen.

Pss. 25:1; 89:47; 132:1; 137:6; Lam. 3:19; 5:1; 2 Cor. 1:5–7

194 *[9/11]* O God, it's been some years since the planes ripped through the buildings, making a holocaust of thousands of people in them, whole burnt offerings or "jump" offerings shattered in pieces on the ground . . . some years since the planes traumatized our psyches, shredded our privileged sense of security, maimed our social networks. Heartstrings still reach out, but are left dangling, because the people we loved are not there. O God, we need your wisdom to move beyond getting even. Give us vision for a wider solution. Convince us all the way down that it won't help to do the same things to somebody else. Through Jesus Christ. Amen.

Lev. 1; Ps. 137:6; Lam. 1:12a; 2:13; 3:19; 5:1; Luke 23:34; Matt. 5:38–48//Luke 6:27–36; Acts 7:60; Rom. 12:14–21

195 Jesus, you know our human feelings. If your family had been tortured, if your village had been gassed, if your women had been raped before they were murdered, wouldn't you at least feel that the world would be a safer place if the perpetrators were dead? For a moment, revenge tastes sweet, the satisfaction that they're going to get a taste of their own medicine. The trouble is, hanging terrorists and rogue rulers won't make the world a safer place. The trouble is, we mock our democratic ideals by not giving them fair trials. Vengeance won't raise the dead or build peace. Jesus, you knew how to live and die for truth and justice while forgiving your enemies. Share your wisdom with government leaders and move in us all to change our hearts. Amen.

Deut. 19:21; Deut. 32:35//Exod. 21:23–24//Lev. 24:19–20; Luke 23:34; Matt. 5:38–48//Luke 6:27–36; Acts 7:60

Admitting to Racism and Prejudice

196 O God, who you are and how you love are really important. Forgive us when we confuse ourselves into thinking that our beliefs and practices are important enough to justify torturing and distorting your image in ourselves and other human beings. Convince us all that your love doesn't depend on creeds and rubrics. Open our eyes to recognize you in every person. Make us flexible to learn from others who are very different from ourselves. Through Jesus Christ. Amen.

Gen. 1:26–30; Jonah passim; Joel 2:28–32; Matt. 15:21–28//Mark 7:24–37; Acts 17:22–31

197 O God, we love our culture—our music and architecture, our literature and style of humor, our ways of cooking food and organizing families and schools and governments. We are truly grateful for many good things about our way of being in the world. But sometimes we're afraid that if too many people who are different from us move into the neighborhood, then what it is to be British or North American or Western European will get lost in customs and practices and languages that we don't like or understand. We're afraid that they'll be

afraid of us, too. And if we fear each other so much, we're bound to be enemies and do terrible things to one another. O God, speak your Word to calm our fears. Open our eyes to recognize one another as your children. Give us courage to open doors and imagination to live together in creative ways. Through Jesus Christ. Amen.

Judg. 2:1–6; Isa. 60:1–6; Acts 10:34–43; 17:22–31

198 O God, you know how easily the idea of manifest destiny captures our imaginations. We want to believe that we are important to you not only as individuals but as a dynasty, race, and culture as well. We read the Bible stories about Israel's election as if they were about us, as an indication that you want us to be exclusively special, as if you want to promote our interests at the expense of others. We want to believe that we are the chosen people, that ours is the land of promise, that we are entitled to lord it over others militarily and economically, culturally and religiously. O God, forgive us for forgetting that we exist to be instruments of your purposes, vehicles of your glory, servants of the servants of God. Forgive us for all of the ways our racism has harmed others. Show us how to make amends. Through Jesus Christ. Amen.

Deut. 7–11; Isa. 60:1–6; Joel 2:1–2, 12–17; Hab. 2:6–20; 1 Pet. 2:9–10

199 O God, the Bible itself insists that religion ought to organize the expression of a person's deepest loyalties. When everybody in a country practices the same religion, it's easy to blur national purpose and religious ideals together. But nowadays, in the United Kingdom, in the European Union, in the United States, we have citizens who are Christian, Jewish, Moslem, Hindu, Buddhist, and Sikh. We worry about how people can be loyal to the same country if they don't worship the same god, or if we all worship you but in such different ways. The

thought crosses our mind that maybe we'd be safer if their religious practices were disallowed. O God, forgive us when our fears and suspicions curtail other people's freedoms. Show us how to be faithful yet tolerant and supportive of other ways of being devoted to you. Through Jesus Christ. Amen.

Judg. 2:1–6; Joel 2:1–2, 12–17; John 4:22–24

200 O God, you are always surprising us. From time to time, you break through our everyday worlds to expose your holiness in ways that are unmistakable. But often, you are there and we miss you, because you contradict our expectations: you keep company with the wrong kind of people; you are party to dubious actions; you insinuate yourself into places where you don't belong. O God, you became human in Jesus to show us: it is your presence that makes things holy. Take away our blindness. Make us watchful to see, alert to spot your work all around. Through Jesus Christ. Amen.

Matt. 11:16–19; Luke 10:25–37; 15; 19:1–10; John 4:1–42; Matt. 9:9–13//Mark 2:13–17//Luke 5:27–32

201 O God, we are full of prejudices. On the outside, we work overtime to disguise it, to treat those who seem different just the same or even better than our own kind. But we catch ourselves when we're going down lonely streets at night and find ourselves more afraid of members of that other race . . . when we wish that they'd just keep quiet, that they'd push their demands for equality later, at some more opportune time . . . when we wish other people would stop talking about it, so that we could forget their suffering . . . when we wouldn't want our children to be one, or to marry one . . . when we insist that if they're going to stay here, they have to dress like us and eat like us and talk like us. O God, forgive our narrowness. Stretch our hearts to recognize your likeness in all your works, and to love your image in all of your children. Through Jesus Christ. Amen.

Ezra 9–10; Neh. 13:23–31; Joel 2:1–2, 12–17; Luke 10:25–37; John 4:1–42

Praying for Peace

202 O God, human tribes and nation-states are good at imitating Jesus in one respect: how often have we come not to bring peace but a sword? Sometimes we come in naked aggression. More often, recently, we tell ourselves we come to bring peace *by* the sword. O God, we're caught in a double bind. We don't know how to secure social order and justice without using force. But when we do, we find ourselves shedding rivers of blood that we didn't intend. O God, forgive us and give us wisdom. Teach us the ways of peace. Through Jesus Christ. Amen.

Joel 2:1–2, 12–17; Matt. 10:34–36; Luke 12:51; 21:16

203 O God, you know that peace is what we really need. But fear and mistrust make us defensive, trigger-happy, so that despite our good intentions we keep on making matters worse. People on the ground need a sense of your presence to feel safe enough to risk not seizing the offensive. Leaders and neighbors need your imagination to discover ways to get along that allow everyone to win. O God, teach us how to be peacemakers. Through Jesus Christ. Amen.

Isa. 2:1–5; Mic. 4:1–5; Matt. 5:9; John 20:21

204 O God, it is a good and pleasant thing when brothers live together in unity. But after decades of ethnic fighting, it's hard to know how to live in peace. How can we trust those people a couple of streets over when we suspect that their gang killed our cousins, even our mother or father, brother or sister? What happens to justice, if we let bygones be bygones? Convince us that there is no future in vengeance. Teach us how to forgive and begin again. Through Jesus Christ. Amen.

Gen. 34; Ps. 133:1; 2 Sam. 2:12–23; 3:26–30; 13

205 O God, it's hard for enemies to work together when we've been at one another's throats for so long . . . when we have turned one another's concessions into new occasions for violence . . . when we're used to seizing every advantage because we expect the other to exact two eyes for an eye, to obliterate a whole village for one soldier's death, to explode random supermarket shoppers with a suicide bomb. We have been too afraid to be trustworthy. We have no reason to trust one another, except that we have no future unless we work for peace. Now is the time, O God, to pour down your wisdom and imagination. Now is the time to loosen our grip on past grievances. Now is the time to show us how to turn again, to rebuild in the here and now. Amen.

Exod. 2:23–24; Lev. 24:19–20; Deut. 19:21; Mic. 4:1–5; Matt. 5:9; John 20:21

206 Send us leaders, O God, who seek your face and rule by your wisdom, who weigh their own desire for power against what is good for the people. Don't let the death of one become the occasion for violent squabbling among would-be successors. Don't let fighting shepherds sacrifice the lambs! Amen.

1 Kgs. 3:3–15; Ezek. 34; John 10:1–18

207 O God, you made us all citizens of Zion, but we thought that meant we could control the turf. We are afraid that there is not enough room or food or shelter in the world for everyone to have enough and to spare. We don't know how to stop fighting over your world. Give us all a sense of your goodness. Reclaim us as your agents. Change our hearts to make us instruments of your peace. Establish your reign of goodwill everywhere. Through Jesus Christ. Amen.

Ps. 87:4–5; Joel 2:1–2, 12–17

208 O God, we rear up our children with such effort. We work to teach them how to be respectful, to empathize with others as fellow human beings. We try to love them, to build all kinds of life skills into them, to provide the kind of education that will be best for them. But then, as a society, we turn the tables, we make a request that must seem very bewildering. Not only do we demand that they risk life and limb for the sake of foreign policy. We require them to do things that run counter to the very values we have taught them: to kill and maim and destroy other human beings. O God, we speak of troop deployment so abstractly. Send your Spirit to enfold our soldiers. Forgive us and our leaders for not counting their costs. Through Jesus Christ. Amen.

Gen. 1:2; Ps. 91:11–12

209 O God, your prophecy of wars and rumors of wars seems to be coming true. How can we enforce peace with war? How can we establish peace among people who don't want peace? Send your Spirit to brood over our chaos. Move in the hearts of all individuals and peoples. Convince us that *you* are our safety. Establish your peace on earth, through Jesus Christ! Amen.

Gen. 1:2; Joel 2:28–29; Mark 13:7

210 O God, it's tricky trying to trace your hand in human history. Bible authors obviously found it more comforting to think you were punishing Israel for her sins than to believe that Babylonian, Assyrian, or Egyptian gods were bigger and tougher than you! They thought you were their god, but that didn't mean you were working to make sure they won all of the battles. What you were really interested in was their developing a national life that embodied your purposes and reflected your glory. O God, the movements of history still baffle us. Give us the wisdom to do and be what you want of us here and now. Through Jesus Christ. Amen.

Isa. 43; Jeremiah passim; Ezekiel passim

211 O God, we call it the Holy Land because it is the land of the prophets and kings we read about in the Bible. But considered as a piece of real estate, it is really very small. Too many people love it, too many people have put down roots in it, because they believe that you live there, and they think they want to be neighbors with you. It's so important to them to be there that they haven't wanted to share it. There's so much blood under the bridge it's hard to see how different groups can learn to trust one another now. O God, you really do live there—among other places. You really do love all of the people who stake out turf there. Give them all a double portion of your wisdom. Serve them all a generous slice of your peace. Through Jesus Christ. Amen.

Pss. 122:6; 133

212 O God, so many people live in war-torn places, in towns and villages where shooting could break out or suicide bombers explode at any time. Every dawn breaks into a day when friends and family members could be killed by accident, on purpose, or on purpose by

accident. Someone ventures out of the house while others get ulcers worrying whether they'll come home. Machine-gun bursts split the air. Blood and bodies crumpled on the street tell them their worst nightmares have come true. O God, envelop them with your presence. Convince them that you are their safety, that you are for them, that your life is their eternal ground. Through Jesus Christ. Amen.

Pss. 7; 13; 27; 31; 46; Isa. 25:6–9

Longing for Good Government

213 O God, you know how hard it is to get people organized so that there is a place for everyone, so that everyone has something useful and satisfying to do. It gets harder when not all of our citizens descend from the same tribe, when even now they have very different customs and values. It gets even harder when some begin to feel so left out as to have no stake in our common life, as to use violence to get even or just to grab what they need. O God, we need your Spirit to enable us to be creative instead of defensive, compassionate rather than vindictive. We need your imagination to dream up a new social order in which everyone has something to gain. Through Jesus Christ. Amen.

Isa. 60:1–6; Ezek. 34

214 O God, you know how easy it is for world leaders to make big decisions whose disastrous consequences they can't anticipate. You know how easy it is for them to "cover up" in an effort to buy more time to make things work out. We know how often the truth is much worse than they realized or we expected. O God,

we need your miracles to keep us from reaping what they have sown. They need humility that acknowledges limits and admits mistakes. Give them wisdom to hesitate, to reconsider, and to make fresh starts. Through Jesus Christ. Amen.

2 Sam. 11–12, 24; 1 Kgs. 21:27–29; Isa. 64:1–9

215 O God, it must be hard to lead a country important enough to play a global role. Trying to understand issues well enough to form an intelligent policy must be taxing even for brilliant minds. Their work is momentous. But sometimes, leaders decide on a plan, commit enormous resources to it, only for everyone else to discover that their assumptions were wrong, their calculations misguided, and their approach ineffective. The trouble is, the leaders themselves have become invested in their mistakes and find it difficult to change their minds. O God, give government officials your wisdom in the first place. But also give them the courage to be honest and the humility to admit it when events prove them wrong. Through Jesus Christ. Amen.

2 Sam. 11–12, 24; 1 Kgs. 21:27–29; Isa. 64:1–9

216 O God, you didn't make us or call us in isolation. You formed yourself a people. Yet you know that when it comes to politics, we aren't very skilled. Corrupt governments at least keep the trains running, but failed states can't seem to get organized at all. O God, fill our leaders with your wisdom and skill. Keep us from opposing our own interests to the common good. Through Jesus Christ. Amen.

1 Sam. 8:4–11, 16–20; 1 Kgs. 2:10–12; 3:3–14; Isa. 9:2–7; 43:18–25; 64:1–9; Jer. 23:1–6; Luke 1:47–55; John 10:1–16; Rom. 13:1–7; 1 Pet. 2:13–17

217 O God, you know we need good governments. You know how difficult it is to weed through special interests and discern what makes for the common good. Give the leaders of the nations hearts to care, eyes to see, and a will to work for what builds up peace and good-will, for what nourishes the weak with the resources of the strong. Through Jesus Christ our Lord. Amen.

1 Sam. 8:4–11, 16–20; 1 Kgs. 9:15–23; Isa. 11:1–10; 64:1–9; Jer. 23:1–6; 1 Tim. 2:2

218 O God, the Bible is full of stories about bad shepherds who slaughter the sheep to feast themselves. And our world is full of corrupt governments and failed states, whose leaders use public office to swell Swiss bank accounts instead of building up their countries. Even in our own nations, politicians are torn between their own power and reputation and facing up to real problems and producing solutions that would do some good. O God, we thank you for the good shepherds who have been faithful in public service. Bless them with a sense of your favor. Raise up more of them so that all the peoples of the world can have the good governments that they need. Through Jesus Christ. Amen.

2 Kgs. 11; Isa. 9:2–7; 11:1–10; Jer. 23:1–6; Ezek. 34; Mic. 5:2–5; 1 Tim. 2:2

219 O God, you know our human slogans. "Power corrupts; absolute power corrupts absolutely." People who have power want to keep it, because it makes them feel big and important, because it enables them to get what they want, because they think they need it to be secure. We who don't have so much of it still feel that "some government—any government—is better than no government," because life would be chaos without one, and chaos might be a fate worse than death. But when

your kingdom comes, there's bound to be a revolution, because utopia will be so different from the societies we invent. O God, help us to trust you more than the present world order. Give us the courage we will need to welcome what is new. Through Jesus Christ. Amen.

1 Sam. 8:4–11, 16–20; Isa. 64:1–9; Matt. 2:1–12; 5–6; Luke 6:20–45; 23:33–43; Col. 1:11–20

220 O God, it happens all the time. Higher-ups give lower-downs the definite impression that they want something done, maybe even that there will be consequences if it isn't done. And then, when the lower-downs carry out their wishes, the higher-ups pretend they had nothing to do with it, even punish the people who did their dirty work for them. O God, you release captives. Give lower-downs caught in such double binds the cunning to survive until you open a way out. Through Jesus Christ. Amen.

2 Sam. 1:1–6; 3:22–39; 18–19

Hungering for Justice

221   O God, we want to put your principles to work in our society, to build infrastructures that will guarantee the necessities of life to everyone and put the good things of life within everyone's reach. But in a country like ours, it's all so complicated. There are so many competing interests, so many entrenched expectations that high ideals and minimal measures are easily set aside. We want to do the right thing until we begin to count the cost. O God, forgive our equivocation. Pardon our lack of perseverance. Fire us up to true repentance that works energetically for reforms. Through Jesus Christ. Amen.

Deut. 14:22–15:23; 24–26; Isa. 1:1, 10–20; 5:1–7; Joel 2:1–2, 12–17; Matt. 5–7; Luke 6:20–38

222   O God, you promised to give a new heart not just to faithful individuals but to whole peoples. Convert nations from greed that grabs what it can get to generosity that gives where there is need; from power that degrades and destroys to energy that builds up and restores; from stupidity that demands simple solutions and quick fixes to imagination that dreams and sees visions of justice rolling down like waters and righ-

teousness like an ever-flowing stream. Through Jesus Christ. Amen.

1 Kgs. 21:1–21; Isa. 1:1, 10–20; 5:1–7; Jer. 31:31–34; Ezek. 36:26–32; Joel 2:1–2, 12–17; Acts 2:42–47; 1 Tim. 6:6–19; Heb. 13:1–8, 15–16

223 O God, it doesn't take prophetic vision to see how our society is headed in many disastrous directions. We burn oil as if there were no tomorrow. We are too greedy to worry about the environment or to pay attention to global warming. We are too afraid and too baffled to give multiculturalism the deeper foundation it needs. We don't care enough to find a way to shelter the homeless on our streets. O God, what we need prophetic vision for is to see to the bottom of social problems and to invent ground-up solutions. We need your wisdom to discern, new hearts to hope, new energy to overcome despair. Through Jesus Christ. Amen.

Isa. 5:1–7; Hab. 2:6–20

224 O God, good and bad events alike expose cracks in our social foundations. Our forebears worked hard to build institutions that would keep us organized and channel resources in life-giving and creative ways. They worked well enough for quite a while. But now we find ourselves in new situations that they weren't designed to handle. We need to remodel the deep structure. O God, you are the cosmic architect and builder. Give us the wisdom and the will to restructure. Through Jesus Christ. Amen.

2 Kgs. 22–23:27; Isa. 1:1, 10–20; 5:1–7; Jer. 2:13; Matt. 7:21–29; Rev. 21

225 O God, we like to think of ourselves as enlightened. We are proud that our countries abolished slavery long ago. Why, then, do we turn a blind eye to

news that it is still practiced in Sudan? in Chinese prisons? in brothels around the world (even in England) where women and children are sold by their families to provide sexual services? in sweatshops staffed by illegal immigrants who work night and day to sew blue jeans? O God, shock us out of our indifference. Make us sensitive to honor your image in all your children. Show us ways to act effectively to bring slavery finally to an end. Through Jesus Christ. Amen.

Gen. 1:26–27; Lev. 25:39–55; Joel 2:1–2, 12–17; Luke 16:19–31

226 O God, we know that our standard of living is very high, but that it is bought at the price of other people's standards of living being very low. Forgive our greed and our sense of entitlement. Raise up economists and leaders clever enough to see and good enough to want to set such unjust systems of distribution right! Through Jesus Christ. Amen.

Deut. 15; 24:19–22; 26:1–15; Isa. 58:1–9; Amos 8:1–12; Exod. 22:25–27; 23:6–10//Lev. 25:8–55; Matt. 19:16–30//Mark 10:17–31//Luke 18:18–30; Acts 2:42–47

227 O God, we're inconsistent. We give lip service to the idea that you created all humans equal. But deep down we need to believe we're better as a hedge against not being good enough. Convince us—each and all—of how much you have always loved us. Forgive the contempt we show to others and our secret contempt for ourselves. Through Jesus Christ. Amen.

Isa. 5:1–7; Joel 2:1–2, 12–17; Luke 15; 18:9–14; John 13:1–17

228 O God, we like to think of ourselves as egalitarian. We put time and effort into organizations that promote equal rights and opportunities for all. But when we get an invitation from someone famous or important, we flirt with self-congratulation. We blush to realize how we really do believe that some people are better than others, how we still hope that associating with higher-ups will "rub off" to make us seem worthier, too. O God, come among us as the Leveler. Show us in no uncertain terms how our real worth comes from keeping company with you. Through Jesus Christ. Amen.

Esth. 5:9–7:10; Luke 14:7–14; John 13:1–17; Matt. 20:20–28//Mark 10:35–45//Luke 22:24–27

229 O God, we live in a rich country. We even live in a conscientious country. We pay reasonably high taxes so that the government will have money to work with. There should be enough in the coffers for everyone to live on. But somehow, we don't get our priorities quite right. For whatever reason, there are still people shivering on our streets. The ones that take refuge in public libraries are being thrown out because they smell. There aren't enough beds or showers in the shelters or bowls of soup on the tables. O God, forgive our lack of follow through. Keep disturbing us until we make good on our resolves. Through Jesus Christ. Amen.

Exod. 22:25–27; 23:6–10; Lev. 25:8–55; Deut. 15:7–11; Ps. 41:1–3; Isa. 58:1–12; Joel 2:1–2, 12–17; Luke 16:19–31; Acts 2:42–47

230 Jesus, you were a wanderer. You slept out under the stars. You had no place to lay your head. Comfort all those who will spend the night without shelter. Protect them from danger. Disturb us and government leaders everywhere with compassion. Mobilize us to provide decent affordable housing for everyone, the world around. Amen.

Gen. 28:15; Ps. 41:1–3; Isa. 58:1–12; Matt. 8:20

231 O God, especially within our group we would like to get along with everybody. When people really care about issues, it feels too uncomfortable to disagree to their face. So we keep quiet, or we muddy the waters whose clarity would stir conflict. The trouble with "going along to get along" is that real people are at stake. They see our silence and wavering as signs that we don't really care about them—worse yet, that you don't really love them either. O God, forgive our cowardice. Give us the courage of our convictions. Give them your comfort to heal their wounds. Through Jesus Christ. Amen.

2 Sam. 11–12; Joel 2:1–2, 12–17; Gal. 2:11–14

232 O God, prisons tend to be miserable places—restrictive, overcrowded, dangerous. After all, they were meant for punishment: if they were too good, they might not seem worth avoiding. And anyway, why should taxpayers fund luxury for people who disrupt our common life? But prisons were also supposed to rehabilitate, and instead they become schools of crime. Prisons can be hell even for the guilty. What about the innocent who were wrongly convicted? O God, forgive our miscarriage of justice and our callousness towards prisoners. Harrow the hell of our prisons. Break down our complacency, and release captives from despair. Through Jesus Christ. Amen.

Ps. 17; Isa. 61:1–2; Luke 4:16–21; Heb. 13:3; 1 Pet. 3:18–20

233 O God, we pray every day for your kingdom to come, but in the meanwhile we have other priorities. We want to make a good living and to stay reasonably healthy. We want to do satisfying work and enjoy a circle of family and friends. Stir us with your compassion. Make us hunger and thirst for a world where everyone has enough and gets to grow into their gifts, where no one is lonely and children are not abandoned, where people are not treacher-

ous because no one is desperate. Bend us with your bias for the worst off, and show us how to help. Amen.

Exod. 22:21–27; 23:6, 9; 1 Kgs. 17:8–16; Matt. 5:6; Matt. 25:31–46; Luke 6:20–31; John 13:1–17; Matt. 6:9–13//Luke 11:2–4; Matt. 6:25–33//Luke 12:22–31

234 O God, sometimes food becomes so scarce and living conditions so dangerous that people move to strange new countries with hopes of finding work. Because they don't know the language or the customs, because sometimes they don't have legal documents, they are easy prey for employers who trap them in a prison of overwork and underpay and their lives become worse than before. O God, inspire government leaders with fresh strategies for helping immigrants and refugees. Give us the determination to end the enslavement and abuse of people already here. Through Jesus Christ. Amen.

Exod. 22:24; 23:9; Deut. 10:19; 14:28–29

235 O God, it's one thing to consider human beings as *individuals*, who make choices, keep promises, build character, develop skills, and strive for goals. What happens when we act in concert is quite another thing. The group seems to be more than the sum of its parts. Its esprit de corps co-opts us into ways of seeing and being in the world, into beliefs about who we and others are, about our rights and privileges and entitlements, without our ever subjecting them to conscious and critical examination. Our whole upbringing and education conspire, and what you see is what you get. What you get is who we are: racist, sexist, Amero-Eurocentrists. O God, open our eyes wide enough to find ourselves guilty. Give us the wisdom to know how to work effectively for social change. Through Jesus Christ. Amen.

Acts 10:1–11:18; Gal. 3:27–29

236 O God, it's hard to imagine what awful lives people must be leaving that they're willing to risk death crossing seas in leaky boats, going through deserts in the back of poorly ventilated trucks, hiding behind trees and bushes, dodging bullets, bribing, falsifying papers, squeezing into cramped quarters, working for slave wages without any legal recourse or protection. They want what we take for granted: safe streets, running water and electricity, schools for their children, health care when they're sick, freedom to choose a career or to practice a religion, an honest day's work for an honest day's pay. O God, we got here first, and we don't always want to share with them. Because we don't understand their language and their customs, we're afraid of them. Remind us that—whether or not we were ever foreigners—we are all guests in your world. Help us to welcome others on your behalf. Through Jesus Christ. Amen.

Exod. 22:21–24; 23:9; Deut. 10:19; 14:28–29

237 O God, the Bible says that there is no point in coming to church, in bowing and scraping, in dotting the liturgical i's and crossing the liturgical t's, unless we love you whole-heartedly and love our neighbors as ourselves. But you know how unjust our society is. You know that for us to live here at all is already to acquiesce in it. Unless we become hermits, we can't come to church without bringing our complicity in social inequities and human suffering along. You also know that however hard we try, we aren't very effective in promoting social reforms. O God, please don't banish us. We can't improve without coming to worship, without repeatedly exposing ourselves to your judgment and wisdom, to your love and power. Through Jesus Christ. Amen.

Amos 5:21–27

Gender Abuse

238 O God, you created both male and female in your image. But some girls and women are trapped in social systems that make them little better than slaves. Some are unwillingly traded into arranged marriages. Many girls do not get to go to school or pursue career interests the way their brothers do. Even in our own culture, many women feel locked in loveless or abusive marriages because they lack job skills that would support a new life. O God, show us how to achieve gender justice on the earth. Through Jesus Christ. Amen.

Gen. 1:26–27; Gal. 3:27–29

239 O God, it happens a lot. A man harasses, sexually abuses, rapes an unwilling woman. But when it becomes known, even the men who disapprove won't do anything about it, because it would compromise collegiality, spoil camaraderie, get in the way of shared projects that are more important to them. Deep down, many enjoy and feel entitled to the conquest. Many participate, or at least acquiesce, in gossip that makes fun of the woman and leaves her reputation in shreds. O God, help us uproot sexism and misogyny in our society. Convince everyone that you love daughters as much as sons. Through Jesus Christ. Amen.

Mic. 6:1–8

240 O God, gay bashing literally happens. Hitler exterminated homosexuals in death camps. Matthew Shepard was tied to a fence, brutally beaten, and left to die out in the cold. Another man was roped to a car bumper and dragged for several miles. But what about menacing graffiti, "fag" jokes and jeers, not only in drunken jock circles but in the "polite" society of well-to-do clubs? What about the evident revulsion that comes over people when they recognize a gay or lesbian couple? What about passionate preachers proclaiming that you hate anything but celibacy and heterosexual marriage? O God, sexuality is core and confusing. Keep us clear that contempt and cruelty never get it right. Through Jesus Christ. Amen.

Mic. 6:1–8

Praying for Prisoners

241 O God, you alone know how many people there are in the world today who suffer for conscience' sake: from those who are merely shunned or denied job promotions to those who are forced into exile or tortured in dark holes of grisly prisons. Thank you for their courage that stays the course, for their loyalty that doesn't waver, for their strength to persevere to the end. Overcome their loneliness with a sense of your presence. Kindle hope with the assurance of your love. Through Jesus Christ. Amen.

Isa. 49:8–16; Matt. 5:10–12; 2 Tim. 2:8–13; Heb. 13:3

242 O God, church-state relations have always been a problem. Already, way back when, rulers half-knew that you are the ruler of the universe and that they were at most vassals created to do your will. But they wanted to think it was the other way around, that you were just a powerful ally who existed to do their bidding. They saw you as a rival whose purposes might run interference with theirs. They reckoned that citizens would be harder to control if they felt more loyalty to you than to the human state. That's why they persecuted prophets and religious fanatics. The Gospels say that's why Jesus was

crucified! All through history, we have kept it up. Why, even in Europe and North America, people were burned alive as heretics and witches. Even now, Moslems are in jail mainly because of their ethnic origin and religious beliefs. O God, forgive us for criminalizing connections with you that differ from our own. Forgive us for the offenses we have committed to defend our states against others' love of your name. Through Jesus Christ. Amen.

Jer. 26:10–24; 37:11–21; 38:4–13; Acts 4:1–4; 5:17–32; 6:8–15; 7:54–60; 2 Tim. 2:8–13

243 O God, we mean to respect your image in every human person. But fear justifies cruelty to others as the price of safety for ourselves. Show us the costs we impose on others. Cut us to the heart with true repentance. Fire us to work for justice. Encourage all prisoners with your love that suffers with them. Give them a taste of your resurrection power. Through Jesus Christ. Amen.

Isa. 49:8–16; Heb. 13:3

244 O God, the temptations of power have always been with us. How convenient—we feel—it would be to get our opponents out of the way. What individuals merely feel, governments and militias all too readily do. Comfort with the strength of your presence those who are imprisoned and tortured. Chisel through rock-hard hearts that mutilate and liquidate other human beings. Set your cross before us to convict us of our bestiality. Give us true repentance that wills and works to bring it to an end. Through Jesus Christ. Amen.

Isa. 49:8–16; John 11:45–53; Matt. 27// Mark 15//Luke 23//John 19; 2 Tim. 2:8–13; Heb. 13:3

245 O God, how many times a day do we turn defensive? How often does our anger boil over against our enemies? How frequently do we compromise, equivocate, or simply turn and run? O God, thank you for the clarity of saints and martyrs. Stir us with their enthusiasm for the gospel. Give us also courage to speak truth to power. Through Jesus Christ. Amen.

Acts 4:13–22; 6–7; 8:1–4; 12:1–19; 14:1–7, 19–23; 16:19–40; 20:17–38; 21–26; 28:17–31; 2 Tim. 2:8–13; Heb. 12:12–29; Rev. 7:13–17

Praying for the Church

246 O God, you are so big and we are so small, your ways so much higher than our ways, that it would be impossible for any human being to get a grip on who you are and what you have in mind all by him- or herself. The Bible shows how you started with Abraham and worked over centuries to educate Israelis into the idea that you were forming them into a people who could advertise your glory and be a channel of your blessing on the whole world. O God, thank you for the church, which brought us up on the story of Jesus, which trained us to be alert to recognize you in Word and sacraments and the world around us, which forms us into people who can advertise who you are and how you love to a confused and broken world. Through Jesus Christ. Amen.

Gen. 12:1–4; 28:10–17; Deut. 7–11; Col. 3; 1 Peter (entire)

247 O God, we don't have to tell you, your church has had its ups and downs. There have been periods of clear proclamation, courageous outreach, sincerity of worship, and faithfulness of life. There have also been seasons of indifference and complacency, of betrayed focus and corruption. Nowadays, the record is mixed, but

the church is still the only institution dedicated to helping people grow in the knowledge and love of God in Jesus Christ. O God, thank you for using our imperfect institutions. Help us to work with you to invent and reform. Through Jesus Christ. Amen.

Pss. 105–106; Acts 15:1–22

248 O God, you call us to be heralds of kingdom coming, to be forerunners who pave the way. But your church has been around for two thousand years. It has settled down and become part of the establishment. We join it because we want to hold on to tradition. O God, forgive us for being reluctant followers. Turn us back into leaders in bringing release to the captive and relief to the oppressed. Through Jesus Christ. Amen.

Luke 10:1–12; Matt. 3:1–12//Mark 1:1–8//Luke 3:1–18//John 1:6–8, 19–28; Matt. 10:1–12//Luke 9:1–6

249 O God, we want to make your kingdom our top priority. We strain and stretch to match our vision and values to yours. The more conscientious we are, the more important this seems. The more important it seems, the greater the urgency to feel that we have got it right, the more desperate our sense that everything depends on making others agree with us. O God, forgive us for forgetting that our church is *your* body, that your body has many organs with different functions, that your house has many rooms, where you work in surprising ways on many things. Help us to get back to our "bit" parts. Free us to be glad that others are doing theirs. Through Jesus Christ. Amen.

Num. 11:4–6, 10–16, 26–30; John 14:1–7; Rom. 12:3–8; 1 Cor. 12:3b–13

250 O God, we want to love you with all that we have and all that we are. We work in the church because we want to put our love into action. But we get distracted, so absorbed with ideas and principles, so caught up in debating what's right and wrong, that we forget to love you above all, to love our neighbors as ourselves, to love our enemies who threaten and oppose many things we hold dear. We dig in against one another and even wish you hadn't called them into your household or made them fellow heirs with us. O God, reach in and reorder our priorities. Stretch our hearts to be wide like yours. Through Jesus Christ. Amen.

Matt. 5:43–48//Luke 6:27–28, 32–36; Matt. 22:34–40//Mark 12:28–34// Luke 10:25–28; 1 Cor. 13

251 O God, missionaries have carried out the Great Commission to preach Jesus Christ in many nations, where the Good News has been translated into a wide variety of cultural shapes and forms. What Christians do in one place can seem incomprehensible to others. O God, you know our flexibility is limited. Keep us from playing Cain to others' Abel. Help us recognize your readiness to accept offerings of many kinds. Through Jesus Christ. Amen.

Matt. 28:18–20; Acts 15:1–22; Gal. 2–3

Caring for the Environment

252 O God, we haven't been very good caretakers. We thought you made the world for us, and we have done our best to use it up ever since. We have cut down trees and overplanted crops. We have dug out coal and burnt oil and polluted the air. We have treated our rivers like flush toilets and thought nothing of contaminating their waters with industrial waste. We got by with it so long as only privileged Europeans and North Americans were in charge of it. But now other countries want to live like we do. They are claiming their right to follow our bad example. If they do—there are so many of them—that will ruin everything! O God, even you must have had second thoughts about leaving human beings in charge. Forgive our self-centered sense of entitlement. Help us to know what to do now. Through Jesus Christ. Amen.

Gen. 1:26–30; Exod. 23:10; Lev. 25:1–7, 18–24; Ps. 8:5–8; Rev. 8–9

253 O God, you call us to know and love your world as you do—at least as much as we can. The challenge of exploring it and making it more hospitable for humans has been our pride and joy. The trouble is that it's all too complicated for us. The things we do to improve and modernize have bad consequences we never dreamed of. They say we're almost in a state of emergency. O God, wake us up to the dangers. Whisper hints into the ears of scientists and social planners. Show us how we should change our ways. Through Jesus Christ. Amen.

Gen. 1:26–30; Exod. 23:10; Job 38–39

254 O God, you loved variety and filled your world with all kinds of things. Open our eyes to honor your likeness in all of them. Make us courteous to allow each a place and time to be and do what you have in mind. Give us wisdom to strike the balance between what humans need and would like to use and the duty to respect the worth of things very different from ourselves. Remind us that there is no need for greed and grabbing, because your Goodness has no bounds. Through Jesus Christ. Amen.

Gen. 1; Lev. 25:1–7, 18–24

255 O God, we have fun picturing Noah and his zoo-laden yacht, tossing on the sea. But the story hits too close to home when it blames global flooding on human imagination gone wrong. We were trying to be creative. How were we to know that aerosol spray cans would poke holes in the ozone layer? Generations felled forests to build houses and roads, to hasten human civilization on its way. We never even thought of global warming or melting ice caps swelling the oceans. O God, your world is fascinating, but our minds are too limited to anticipate important consequences. You told Noah how to build the ark. Give us wisdom to know what to do now. Through Jesus Christ. Amen.

Gen. 6:11–7:24; Job 38–39; Rev. 8:7; 9:13–19

256 O God, scientists say we are mostly made of water: it makes our foods juicy and is the starter

ingredient in our drinks. Scientists say that we grow from seeds in a bag of water and are then squeezed into the world when the balloon bursts. The Bible tells us we are reborn through water as your daughters and sons. Science and religion ought to convince us that water is precious. They strongly suggest that you want us to take good care of our water supplies. O God, forgive our indifference. Make us good stewards of water. Through Jesus Christ. Amen.

Ezek. 47:1–12; Rev. 8:8–11; 22:1–2

257 O God, getting water right has always been a tricky thing. Too little, and crops shrivel up, animals die of thirst, clans start moving in to seize others' better-irrigated land. Too much water, and the created order dissolves, whole towns and fields get washed away, people and livestock drowned. However much modern engineering helps, it is still true: the primal forces of nature are too much for us. We can't control the weather, and we haven't learned how to prevent floods. O God, be with those whose homes and lives are threatened. Strengthen the rescue workers to protect them. Give us all compassion to help and the will to rebuild. Through Jesus Christ. Amen.

Gen. 6:11–13; 7:11–24; Exod. 17:1–7; Job 38:8–11; Isa. 35:1–10; Ezek. 47:1–12; Rev. 12:13–17; 22:1–2

258 O God, we thank you for not creating us for chaos. We are glad that you made us in a world with regularities that we can more or less discover and count on—to grow food, to devise shelter, to feel safe enough to decorate your world with designs of our own. O God, keep reminding us that we are guests, not owners. Don't let us forget that our understanding is limited. Hold back our urges to dominate and destroy. Through Jesus Christ. Amen.

Gen. 1; Ps. 104

SCRIPTURE INDEX

The numbers listed in the index refer to the prayer number, not the page number.

INDEX OF THEMES

The numbers listed in the index refer to the prayer number, not the page number.